RAILWAYS and TRAN
of
HAMMERSMITH & WEST LONDON

by Frank Goudie and Douglas Stuckey

Contents

FORGE BOOKS
55 Brookside
Wokingham
Berks

ISBN 0 904662 25 X

Front cover: The bottom painting ''The Train, Bedford Park'' by
Camille Pissarro (1897 oil) is reproduced by kind permission of the private owners.

Hammersmith at the end of the nineteenth century.

Travelling Hopefully

"Hammersmith" – "the most western of the Inner London boroughs it seems to have derived its name from two Anglo-Saxon words meaning 'hammer' and 'smithy'," says The London Encyclopaedia. There is a charm about the amiable simplicity of this explanation of the name's derivation. For centuries Hammersmith was merely a tiny hamlet adjunct to Fulham, but always it lay in the path of the most ancient routes from the Capital to Bristol and Bath, the West and Wales. It was a place through which men "travelled hopefully" rather than arrived. Set by a then much broader, shallower, meandering Thames it was an area of high fertility and its market gardens were famous. Standing now by the "crowded rumbling" streets which carry the burden of the Flyover, it is pleasant to read of "orchards of apples, pears, cherries, plums and walnuts, with raspberries and gooseberries between fruit trees, and some glass-houses for pineapples and grapes . . ." By 1879 when the railways had taken 128 acres of land and the housing and industrial building which followed the rails was booming, agriculture still held its own in several districts. Slightly earlier when the Birmingham, Bristol and Thames Junction Railway put up for sale land at Eynham Farm which was surplus to their requirements, they advertised: "it abounds with brick earth of the highest character, with an average depth of 8½ feet, the substratum is gravel . . . and immense income will be derivable from the land arising out of the vast number of sheep and cattle from Northamptonshire (by the Railways) and the West of England, which would need a place for repose the night antecedent to the market." Good brickfields were another feature of burgeoning Hammersmith. As late as 1878, William Morris chose to live in Kelmscott House by the river, "the situation is certainly the prettiest in London", he wrote to his wife.

By 1801 Hammersmith's population had reached 5,600, by 1851 12,000, it rocketed to 150,000 between the two world wars and started a decline after 1945. As we have said Hammersmith was an adjunct to Fulham where the Bishop of London's palace was situated. Fulham and Hammersmith remained united for administrative purposes until 1900 when the Metropolitan boroughs of Fulham and Hammersmith were established, each with a mayor, alderman and councillors. Sir Walter Besant in his "Survey of London, North of the Thames", published in 1911 makes an interesting perambulation of the borough boundaries:

"Hammersmith is bounded on the south by Fulham and the river, on the west by Chiswick and Acton, and on the east by Kensington. Until 1834 it was incorporated with the parish of Fulham, and on Ascension Day of that year the first ceremony of 'beating the bounds' took place. The West London Railway runs in the bed of an ancient stream which rose north of Wormwood Scrubs and ended at Chelsea Creek, and this brook was crossed by a bridge at the place where the railway bridge (Addison Bridge) now stands on the Hammersmith Road. The stream was evidently the determining factor in the old parish boundary line between Kensington and Hammersmith, but Hammersmith borough includes the line in its course from Willesden to Uxbridge Road, going beyond it to the Harrow Road and Kensal Green Cemetery at the north end; further south it runs out in an irregular loop to include Latimer Road Station, returning to the railway at Uxbridge Road; subsequently it dips just westward of the railway to Hammersmith Road. On the south side the boundary line marches with Fulham – that is to say, westward along the Hammersmith Road as far as St. Paul's School, where it dips southward to include the school and grounds, and thence to the river by Yeldman and Chancellor Roads. From here it proceeds midway up the river to a point almost opposite the end of Chiswick Ait, then northward up British Grove as far as Ravenscourt Gardens, almost due north to within a few yards of the Stamford Brook Road; it follows the trend of that road westward to the North and South-Western Junction Railway. It crosses the railway three times, going northward until it is on a level with Jeddo Road. It then turns eastward, cuts across the north of Jeddo Road to Wilton Road West. Northward it runs to the Uxbridge Road, follows this eastward for a few yards, and strikes again northward up Old Oak Road and Old Oak Common Road, until it reaches Wormwood Scrubs public and military ground. It then trends north-eastward, curves back to meet the Midland and South-Western Line as it crosses the canal, and follows Old Oak Common Road until on a level with Willesden Junction Station, meets the western Kensington boundary, running between the Roman Catholic and Protestant Cemeteries at Kensal Town. Thus the complete circuit of the Borough has been indicated.''

Our little book does not claim to follow borough boundaries entirely for its contents; it largely excludes Willesden Junction which administratively has been a part of Hammersmith, but whose vastly important transport structure and connections relate principally east, north and west to other places and people.

Before the development of railways and other transport encouraged the speculator builder the needs of a large labour force for the actual construction work had led to some new housing. Cottages appeared on boggy ground near Brook Green, to be occupied by Irish labourers working for the West London Railway and for the brickfields near at hand. Some early housing was primitive and by 1856 only 2000 houses had piped water. The opening of the Hammersmith and City line in 1864 accelerated development and the stations at Ladbroke Grove and Goldhawk Road were planted in open fields, but encouraged in the usual Metropolitan way speculators were soon abroad buying out smallholders, and providing solid but affordable homes for the burgeoning lower middle classes. The area of Shepherds Bush was plastered with two and three-storey terraces and small shops, and ownership was assisted by building society mortgages. A flow of new residents into Hammersmith about the middle of the 19th century also arose from the great slum clearance programmes of the Metropolitan Board of Works in the squalid purlieus of the old centre of London. A variety of enterprises came westwards at the turn of the century e.g. the precursors of the M O Vale Company at Brook Green, and Joseph Lyons who came to Cadby Hall, just to the west of Addison Road railway bridge, taking over what had been the pianoforte works of Charles Cadby whose ''Cadby'' name was retained for the products of the famous caterers who revolutionised the food industry.

As London boomed and bustled so did Hammersmith. It was as a world of entertainment that Hammersmith's name and fame travelled most memorably – a popular vantage point for the Varsity boat race; Ideal Homes exhibitions and shows at Olympia (on its border); Joe Loss and the crooning, twisting, swinging and bopping at the Palais, drama of a sterling quality at the Lyric, Lime Grove studios as well as the Wood Lane TV Centre for the burgeoning television. ''Every London taximan used to

4

know the 'Red Cow' and the restaurants along the Broadway'', as Philip Witting began his revised "A History of Hammersmith" in 1965.

With all its industry and its leisure popularity and the floodtide of increasingly mobile Londoners passing through, problems of traffic approached the intolerable. An early attempt at a solution came when the first part of Western Avenue was constructed westward from Wood Lane in 1921 (but did not reach Denham until 1943). The post war decision to link Western Avenue closer to the centre of London by the building of Westway led to some of the first "Roads v People" battles, sparked by sympathy for unhappy residents forced now to live under a concrete viaduct or alongside a speedway from which a fog of pollution continually poured down onto them. Similarly in 1925 work started on the initial section of the Great West Road from Chiswick through Brentford and Hounslow. Here again the last miles to be built were those taking the Great West Road towards the heart of London and including in 1961 the Hammersmith Flyover taking traffic high to the south of the Broadway and noisily divorcing the Broadway from the River.

Hammersmith Broadway in 1911 – LCC tramcar on route 82 bound for 'Near Willesden Junction' and General 'K' type buses.

Hammersmith and Fulham Archives and Local History Collection

LNWR steam railmotor car at Woodstock Road halt.

Lens of Sutton

Level crossing on Bath Road in 1933. On the right is 62 Bath Road, home of Lucien Pissarro.

Hounslow Cultural and Community Studies –
Local Studies Collection Chiswick Library

Rear of Hammersmith and Chiswick station – desolation after closure, but the tree survived for many years.

J. E. Connor

North and South West Junction – A Long Way Round

A major benefit expected from early railways around London was swift connection with the metropolis, but their tracks seemed to have an inclination to bolt off in a tangential, if not wholly opposite direction, resulting in long, unwanted if leisurely rambles across the countryside.

Hammersmith's first railway came in a sweeping arc from the west/north west, a branch from South Acton on the North and South West Junction Railway to "Hammersmith Station" which was, in fact, located on Chiswick High Road where Ravensmede Way now runs and just outside the borough boundary a mile to the west of Hammersmith Broadway.

The construction of the branch had been authorised by the N & SWJ's directors outside of the company's guaranteed capital, and a later inquiry by a committee of shareholders said it could find no reason nor likely source of traffic for the project – and time did not modify their adverse judgement!

The branch was opened for mineral traffic on 1 May 1857 and for passengers on 8 April 1858. In July 1880 the terminus was renamed more appropriately "Hammersmith and Chiswick": the "West London Observer", which used to publish railway time-tables referred to the station as the North London Station at Turnham Green. It was, in fact, closer to Chiswick village than the Chiswick station on the Hounslow loop. The initial passenger service was 9 trains on weekdays, 5 on Sundays, to and from Acton Gate House Junction, and hauled by the NSWJR's first and only steam engine, a Sharp Stewart 0-4-0 saddle tank which was stabled in a tiny shed near the terminus near Gate House Junction. It had a long and varied career, being absorbed into NLR locomotive stock and rebuilt at Bow in 1872 as an 0-4-2ST with a 3-ton steam crane, in which form it lasted for another 79 years. The "train", a single composite coach, was treated in a somewhat cavalier fashion when it was being joined to or detached from an NLR "main liner" at the junction, often being released in the down direction by snatching at the coupling whilst the NLR train merely slowed in its circuitous tour of North London from Fenchurch Street via Stepney, Bow, Hackney, Islington and Kilburn!

The shareholders' anger at the building of the "Hammersmith" branch was understandable but the facilities provided were hardly elaborate. The terminus was a converted existing two-storey house on the main road, with a single long platform accessed through the garden at the rear.

The NSWJR had no rolling stock of its own and came under the management of the NLR in 1860 who provided the necessary stock and motive power. In 1871 it was leased to the LNWR, Midland and NLR jointly but the NLR continued to service its operation.

From 1 November 1865 the branch train began to run through to Acton (now Acton Central) after reversal at Gate House. On 1 January 1880, coincident with the opening of South Acton station the Hammersmith trains, now slightly less poverty-stricken three 4-wheeled coaches hauled by an NLR 4-4-0T, ran into and terminated at a bay platform for interchange with the rest of the NLR.

On 4 January 1909 an LNWR 48-seater steam rail motor, nicknamed locally 'Little Jenny'' was introduced on the branch; more than enough to meet the needs of this sparsely-used byway. In April of the same year intermediate halts were opened at Rugby Road, Woodstock Road and Bath Road and at the terminus a raised wooden platform with a canopy was provided to facilitate access to the rail motor, but simultaneously the booking office was closed. Tickets were then issued by a conductor/ guard. On 9 March 1913 an LNWR petrol-electric rail-motor No 9 replaced ''Little Jenny'' but these changes did little to add profit or popularity and on 1 January 1917 all the branch stations were closed and passenger services ceased. For the last thirty years of its life the Branch had provided a roughly half-hour interval service on weekdays and on Sunday afternoons after a late start and the usual ''church interval'', which was observed right up to the Great War. Also, the NLR appeared to have little interest in an early morning workmen's traffic, since from the 1870's to 1914 the first train rarely ran before 7.45 am.

However, the line had been known for a time as ''Soapsuds Alley'' when it was used by laundry workers travelling to ''Soapsuds Island'' (South Acton). One wonders sometimes whether some of these local epithets were journalistic rather than popular parlance.

Freight had been marginally more successful, needing two daily trains to serve the coal sidings at the terminus and Eastman's Dye and Cleaning Works and an asphalt plant near the Gate House Junction. By the Bath Road level crossing (which often caused frustration as it remained closed during shunting operations at the terminus goods sidings) and behind the signal box was the one-time home of the French Impressionist, Lucien Pissarro, No 62 Bath Road.

Lucien's father, Camille, and other members of the family painted the immediate vicinity (which they always styled Bedford Park, although it was rightly Stamford Brook). The first floor railed balcony must have formed an ideal place for quiet observation of comings and goings on the little branch.

This was in many ways a cosmopolitan community and an accident on 23 December 1875 at Woodstock Road level crossing had resulted earlier in the death of Sergey Kravchinsky, known as ''Stepniak'', a Russian writer and revolutionary, alleged to have been the assassin of the Chief of the Tsarist Secret Police. Apparently, there was a footpath crossing only at this point, as the driver of the train which hit ''Stepniak'' has referred to him: ''absent-mindedly climbing over the stile''. The inquest verdict included a rider: ''the attention of the railway company should be called to the necessity of providing a bridge over the crossing and that, pending its erection, a man should be stationed to warn pedestrians of approaching trains'', not a demanding post! In fact, in due course, a bridge was built.

Freight services struggled on for many years. By the summer of 1957 all that remained was a Monday, Tuesday and Thursday only train leaving South Acton in late morning calling at Parry's Wharf, Acton coal depot, arriving at Hammersmith at 12.25, departing thence at 3.40 pm and shown working through to Kew Bridge.

In its final years the branch was worked as an unstaffed siding with a 10 mph speed limit. From what had been a near monopoly by ex-LNW 0-8-0s, a variety of motive power was seen, including D 8000 diesels and Fowler ''Crab'', Ivatt 4MT and BR Standard 2-6-0s as well as Stanier Class 5 4-6-0s. An RCTS Special visited the line on 10 November 1956 hauled by BR 2-6-4T No. 80065.

Within 12 years of opening the Branch was crossed just north of its Hammersmith terminus by a viaduct carrying LSWR and (later District) trains to points west from a station hard by Hammersmith Broadway. The self-evidently popular and useful service which they provided emphasised the redundancy of the railway below, whose auguries were never propitious.

Final closure of the branch came on 2 May 1965, a predictable spin-off from the Beeching investigations.

In 1996 the track and level crossing gates of the NSWJR were removed. The future of the released land provoked lively controversy. Proposals for shops, bowling alleys and supermarkets came (and went) as did the intention to build an extension to Chiswick Polytechnic. Eventually land was sold to Notting Hill Housing Trust and 31 homes were completed in 1996.

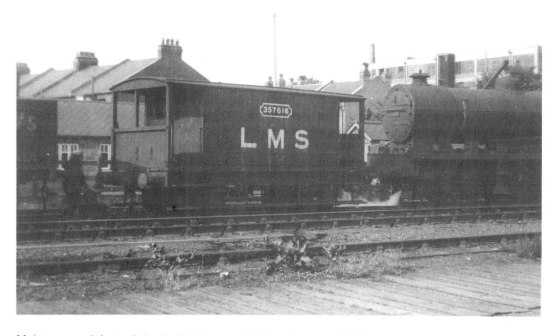

Maintenance of the track for the final years of freight only was probably minimal and this brake van has derailed just outside the terminus.

Lens of Sutton

The scene of the accident on the Hammersmith and City extension railway, near Kensington Park: Workmen digging the ruins of the fallen viaduct for their buried comrades. (From Illustrated News, 15 Nov. 1862).

The Hammersmith
& City Railway

The Great Western Railway's Paddington terminus was too remote from the City for the company to contemplate developing London residential traffic, but when the Metropolitan Railway was opened from Farringdon Street to Bishops Road, Paddington on January 10 1863 it served as a useful extension of the GWR, being worked by that company with broad gauge trains. It became possible for Great Western trains from the western suburbs to reach the important business district of the City's Square Mile, and it became feasible to tap the developing business traffic north of Hammersmith, where suburban housing, hitherto slow in growth, was now burgeoning. So in company with the Metropolitan and in anticipation of the Met's opening, the Great Western joined in supporting a Bill for a branch 2 miles 33 chains long from a junction with the GWR main line at Green Lane, near Westbourne Park, to Hammersmith.

For its part, the Metropolitan was interested in winning traffic from the growing residential districts of Notting Hill, Shepherds Bush and Hammersmith, and a connection could be provided between Paddington and the recently opened outlet to the south via the West London Extension Railway, (a spur from the Hammersmith & City line at Latimer Road to the West London Railway at Addison Road was also included in the H & C's plans).

Powers for the line were granted by the Hammersmith & City Railway Act of July 22, 1861. The Chairman was R. J. Smith, and John Fowler was appointed Engineer at a fee of £8,825. In March 1862 W. A. Wilkinson and John Parson, the Met Chairman and Deputy Chairman, joined the H & C Board, Parson soon being involved in speculative advance purchases of land through which the new railway was to pass. The contract for building the line was awarded to Francis Rummens of 3 Green Square, Westminster, the price of £223,500 to include the purchase of land, and the branch, 39 chains in length, from Latimer Road to the West London Railway near Uxbridge Road Station. Also included were the construction of three stations and the maintenance of the railway for 12 months. The line was double track, of mixed gauge, and would initially be worked by the Great Western. The contract was signed on June 29 1862, Rummens agreeing to accept £168,000 of his fee in H & C shares. Construction went ahead, and Colonel Yolland, Royal Engineers, inspected the line for the Board of Trade on May 16 1864; flat-bottomed rails weighing 69lb per yard and 16ft 9ins long were secured to cross sleepers by fang bolts and wood-screws. There were 12 underbridges and 2,958 yards of the line were carried on brick viaduct; this was necessary because there were no cuttings and consequently little spoil was available for embankments. In evidence before a House of Commons Select Committee on March 14 1864 Ritchie, the Surveyor, said that 21 houses in Hammersmith parish and 5 in Chiswick parish had been purchased to make way for the new railway.

Intermediate stations were at Shepherds Bush and Notting Hill (now Ladbroke Grove). Colonel Yolland was unable to recommend the opening of the railway because some wrought-iron girders would not be strong enough to bear the weight of 8 or 9 tons on the driving wheels of the GWR engines, the permanent way at the junction with the branch to the West London Railway was not finished, and some embankments were showing signs of subsidence. However, the railway was inspected again on June 13 and found satisfactory, and from that day a GWR broad gauge train service ran every half-hour between Hammersmith and Farringdon Street. From July 1 there were Great Western trains at half-hour intervals from Addison Road (now Kensington (Olympia)); these were joined up with or uncoupled from the Hammersmith trains at Notting Hill. On weekdays the first train left Hammersmith at 7.30 am, and the last one arrived back there at 11.00 pm; journey time was 38 minutes.

The connecting line to the West London Railway at Uxbridge Road Junction was opened on July 1 1864 from Latimer Road Junction; a station called Latimer Road was opened on December 16 1868. This connection was closed by bomb damage on October 20 1940 but not finally abandoned until March 1 1954.

The locomotives used on the H & C services were broad gauge 2-4-0 tank engines specially designed for the GWR by Daniel Gooch, and also used on Metropolitan trains between Bishops Road and Farringdon Street; they were the only broad-gauge engines designed for the GWR to have outside cylinders, rendered necessary in order to leave room for condensing tanks between the frames. The Hammersmith & City trains were causing congestion for the GWR between Paddington and Westbourne Park, so on October 30 1871 two additional tracks on the north side, 2 miles 79 chains long, were provided for the H & C trains; these were built by the GWR and leased to the Hammersmith & City. At the same time, Westbourne Park station, originally just south of the junction with the Great Western main line, was resited at the junction itself, and a station was opened as an island platform, serving the H & C tracks only, at Royal Oak, about a mile from Paddington. This entailed Hammersmith & City trains crossing the GWR tracks on the level; this was severely frowned on by the Board of Trade and a fly-under was provided from May 12 1878, the H & C agreeing to pay the GWR £25,000 for their share of the work.

The Great Western and the Metropolitan had no financial interest in the Hammersmith & City Railway but worked together amicably in operating it, once a serious dispute over allocation of shares in the Met extension to Moorgate, and the Metropolitan's desire for a more frequent service between Bishops Road and Farringdon Street which had resulted in the GWR withdrawing its trains in August 1863, had been put behind them. On November 24 1864 the Great Western proposed that they should lease the Hammersmith & City in perpetuity from December 31, taking over all loans and preference shares. During the previous half-year 1,270,140 passengers had been carried, exclusive of season tickets, despite the GWR's refusal to open the stations at Notting Hill and Shepherds Bush, though the H & C Board considered that they had been ready since mid-August.

On February 2 1865 the Hammersmith & City put forward an alternative plan, that the line should be transferred jointly to the Great Western *and* the Metropolitan, the two companies paying a dividend of 5% on the whole ordinary share capital for the year ending December 31 1865, this gradually increasing until it reached 5 1/2% four years later, and then continuing at that figure. This proposal was ratified by the H & CR Board, by the Metropolitan's Act of June 19, 1865 and the GWR Act of July 15 1867. It took effect from July 1 1867; the line had already been operated by a joint committee since June 1 1865. The train service from Hammersmith to the City was worked by Metropolitan standard gauge trains from April 1 1865, while the Great Western removed the broad gauge metals from the H & CR between Hammersmith and Latimer Road in August 1868 and between Uxbridge Road and Westbourne Park on 15 March 1869; thenceforth GWR trains were standard gauge.

One reason for the modest station initially provided at Hammersmith was the H & C's plan to extend their line to Richmond, for which extension the Hammersmith and City Railway Junction Bill was submitted in 1864. At a meeting of the House of Commons Select Committee on 14 March, Myles Fenton the Met's new General Manager was questioned by Gathorne Hardy in the Chair:

"Since the Met line has been opened, notwithstanding the shortness of the line there has been a very enormous traffic?".

"Yes, we carry about 10,000,000 passengers a year in round numbers."

"The railway runs from Paddington up to Farringdon Street does it not?"

"Yes."

"Have you considered the H & C Junction Railway in relation to your Met Rly traffic?"

"Yes, I have. We expect a very large traffic from the Hammersmith line to come upon our Metropolitan Railway . . .

There will be a very large traffic from Richmond, the residents of Richmond come into the City daily. We should then have complete access to the City, either at Farringdon Street or Finsbury, and there will be considerable traffic on the whole length of the line, Richmond, Kew, Turnham Green and Hammersmith. I expect that the whole of the district will be crowded with a population who would require to go to the City and return. But the greatest advantage, I think would be to the poorer classes in the districts on our line, the districts of Clerkenwell, Kings Cross, St Pancras and all that district north of London where there are vast numbers of poor persons. I think it would be of great value to them to be able to get out to Kew and Richmond."

"Kew Gardens I think would be the favourite resort of the people."

"They (the Great Western) worked your line for a considerable period did they not?"

"Yes, until 10 August last."

"You differed."

"Our attention is solely devoted to the accomodation of Metropolitan traffic. The GWR have a thousand miles of railway in the Country to attend to, and their officers could not devote all to our line, which ours can . . . The Great Western have very little suburban traffic on their lines, and the number of trains which they run was in my opinion too small to develop the traffic there."

"Though you look to the Great Western to work the H & C line?"

"I do not know that they are going to work it."

Hammersmith train at Latimer Road in March 1901 hauled by 'A' Class 4-4-0T No 24.

6 car train of 1906 saloon stock in original varnished teak and white livery.

Train for New Cross (LBSCR) at Hammersmith 1917. The Great War has brought women booted and eager to replace men on active service.

However, the extension failed in favour of the London and South Western Railway's Kensington and Richmond line from Addison Road on the West London Railway to Richmond, opened in 1869, and in August 1864 plans were laid to rebuild Hammersmith station.

To accommodate the Great Western's desire to reach Richmond they were given running powers over the Kensington and Richmond line from a junction at Grove Road, Hammersmith, and the LSWR was required to lay broad gauge rails should they be requested by the GWR, though this was not exercised.

The spur at Grove Road was used for a short-lived Great Western service from Bishops Road to Richmond, from June 1 to October 31 1870. From October 1 1877 the Metropolitan began running between Aldgate (to which their line had been extended in 1876) and Richmond, using their famous Beyer Peacock 4-4-0 tank engines and "rigid-eight" coaches. In 1894 the GWR service was resumed and henceforth Metropolitan and Great Western trains could be seen at Richmond until the Hammersmith & City line was electrified in 1906, after which it was replaced by a service of GWR rail-motors between Richmond and Notting Hill, but this was discontinued in 1910.

In March 1869 an engine shed was built at Hammersmith at a cost of £1,569 by Brassey & Co.; in 1884 this was shared by Metropolitan "B" Class 4-4-0T Nos 51 to 66 and a number of GWR 2-4-0 tank engines.

When the LSWR built their line from Addison Road to Richmond in 1869 the H and CR terminus at Hammersmith had to be relocated a short distance further south. Brassey & Co. built the new station, and a station at Latimer Road, near the junction with the line to Uxbridge Road and the West London Line, was erected by the same contractor and opened on December 16 1868.

Horse bus services from Hammersmith were operated by contractors for the H & CR, to Barnes (1878 to 1899) and to Turnham Green (1875 to 1878). On August 25 1878 promoters of a street tramway between Hammersmith and Barnes asked if the Hammersmith & City would be agreeable to such a scheme, but the Joint Committee decided that beyond keeping an eye on any further developments, no action was necessary at that time.

On July 21 1880 the Joint Committee decided to widen the line to four tracks, but, not surprisingly, this suggestion was never carried out; as most of the H & CR was built on viaduct quadrupling would have been very expensive and it seems doubtful, anyway, if the traffic would have warranted it.

A Bill for an Acton & Hammersmith Railway, opposed by the GWR and the Metropolitan, had been thrown out by the House of Lords early in 1874. In the same year a scheme for a railway from Shepherds Bush to join the authorised Hounslow & Metropolitan Railway was discussed and the H & C's engineer was instructed to prepare a rough estimate of its cost, but subsequently the Joint Committee decided not to proceed with this project. Another projected line from Hammersmith to Fulham was planned in 1875, but the Bill for this was withdrawn after arrangements regarding fares were agreed with the District Railway, who had powers for the same route.

A branch from Latimer Road on the H & CR to Acton was authorised by an Act of 1882, granted to a nominally independent company, and some construction began at the Acton end in the following year. The Metropolitan and the GWR agreed to work the line jointly, but the scheme failed to raise the necessary capital and was abandoned. Similarly, a line from Wood Lane on the H & CR to Acton (the West Metropolitan

Railway), to be worked by the H & CR with a shuttle service, failed to attract the needed investment and was abandoned in 1904.

Special events at Earls Court brought extra traffic to the Hammersmith & City; for the German Exhibition in May 1891 and the Industrial Exhibition three years later special trains at cheap fares were run via Latimer Road and the West London Railway to the District station at Earls Court.

As the Metropolitan Railway extended eastwards the City terminus of trains from Hammersmith advanced; to Moorgate in 1865, to Liverpool Street in 1875. From February 1 1875 Hammersmith trains ran into Liverpool Street Great Eastern Railway station, where they had the use of one platform. When the Met was extended to Bishopsgate on July 12 1875 their trains ceased to run into the GER station; the junction was taken out in 1907. Aldgate was reached by Metropolitan metals on November 11 1876, when this became the terminus for H & C trains. As part of the Metropolitan & District Railways (City Lines and Extensions) Act a line jointly owned by the two companies was opened from Aldgate to join the East London Railway at Whitechapel. The Act, dated August 11 1879, also authorised a curve from St Mary's Junction to Whitechapel Junction on the ELR, and this made it possible for trains from Hammersmith H & CR to be extended over the East London to New Cross (South Eastern) station; this service commenced on October 6 1884, which was also the date when the final link in the Inner Circle between Mansion House and Aldgate, which had caused much dissension between the Met and the District was opened.

On August 1 1872 a half-hourly service of trains, operated by the GWR, began running from Moorgate (but from Bishopsgate from July 12 1875 and from Aldgate from December 4 1876) to Mansion House, via the H & CR the Latimer Road curve, the West London Railway and the District Railway at Earls Court. This was known as the Middle Circle, though it fell short of being a true circle by the gap of about a half-mile between Aldgate and Mansion House stations.

On November 11 1902 Gates, the Metropolitan's Engineer, wrote to Ellis, his General Manager, to say that the H & CR station at Hammersmith was in a very poor condition, with rotting timbers and roofs nearing collapse; the GWR had already stated that urgent action was necessary. Tenders were invited, and the contract for building a new station was awarded to William Walkerdine & Co of Derby in September 1907, for the sum of £12,939, the subcontractor for steel and ironwork being Cross & Cross of Walsall. In addition to the existing 13ft wide platform, two more island platforms 16ft wide were planned, and construction was in red, brindled and Staffordshire brick, with facings of hard Yorkshire and Patent Victoria stone.

Work began in January 1908; the station was designed by P. E. Culverhouse, the Great Western's architect. A more spacious concourse was created by setting back the tracks. The street frontage, with a small cab yard, has a large clock on a pediment, with a full-width iron and glass canopy, which carried the legend "Great Western & Metropolitan Railways Hammersmith" in bold letters; for good measure the same lettering was carried on the curved central front elevation. The total cost of the new station was £20,410.

The wooden buildings at Notting Hill & Ladbroke Grove station also badly needed renewal, and a new station was built in 1902 at a cost of £13,836; this was renamed Ladbroke Grove (North Kensington) in 1919, and became plain "Ladbroke Grove" under London Transport in 1938. It is a substantial building in red brick with stone window sills and facings; the steel and glass canopies are both supported on pillars and cantilevered out from the station walls.

Until 1900 the Hammersmith & City Railway had been reasonably successful financially, but from that year onwards its takings began to be seriously depleted owing to competition from the Central London Railway and the London United Tramways which electrified its routes in the Hammersmith – Shepherds Bush area in 1901. For the H & CR itself to be electrified seemed the only remedy to combat the loss of traffic. The Metropolitan readily accepted this, and managed to persuade the Great Western to follow suit. The change to electric traction was authorised by the Metropolitan Railway Act of July 31 1902, and tenders for the supply of electric rolling stock were invited, the contract going to the Metropolitan Amalgamated Railway Carriage & Wagon Co. for provision of 20 6-car trains, with electrical equipment by British Thompson Houston. The cars were of the open saloon type with end doors, consisting of 3rd class motors, and 3rd class and 1st/3rd class composite trailers. Control equipment was of BTH GE76 type and each motor car had four 150hp traction motors.

The total cost of the 20 trains, £254,903, was shared equally between the Metropolitan and the Great Western, the whole electrification scheme being a joint enterprise of the two companies. Ownership of the trains themselves was also joint, and this was reflected in the lettering they carried, which very tactfully showed ''Great Western & Metropolitan Railways'' on one side and ''Metropolitan & Great Western Railways'' on the other. The livery was Metropolitan varnished teak with cream waist and fascia panels; they carried a rather ugly ''H & C'' monogram, and the motor cars had roller destination blinds at their ends. In 1908 it was decided to split the trains into two 3-car units for off-peak working, which entailed equipping the two middle cars of each train with driving apparatus, brakework fittings, destination blinds etc., and fitting the composite trailers with partitions to provide separate smoking and non-smoking accomodation for the first class passengers. Once again the cost was divided equally between the parent companies, and the first train to be so converted went into service on February 2 1908. From 1911 onwards sliding centre doors were fitted at Neasden, concurrently with similar modifications being carried out on the Met's own 1904/5 saloon cars.

Electric working began on November 5 1906 with one train, and by December 3 four additional trains were operating between Hammersmith and Aldgate, and four between Addison Road and Aldgate. Withdrawal of steam trains apart from through trains to Richmond was completed on January 19 1907.

The work of converting the H & CR was carried out by the GWR with their own labour, using steel conductor rails supplied by Frodingham Iron & Steel Co., porcelain insulators by Doulton & Co. and cable connections and rail bonds by W. T. Henly's Telegraph Works. As with the Metropolitan and District conversions, separate positive and negative conductor rails were employed, with traction current at 600 volts d.c. The Great Western constructed a 6,000kW power station at Park Royal, and there were substations at Old Oak Common, Royal Oak and Shepherds Bush.

The contract for new electric car sheds at Hammersmith was given to Messrs Walkerdine of Derby for £31,172; with the permanent-way therein to cost a further £11,897. As the purchase of land for the new depot had been expensive, the depot, which was 1,000ft long, proved a costly item. It was opened in 1906, and a year later the old engine shed at Hammersmith was demolished. The car sheds were situated on the east side of the running lines and just north of the station; they were equipped with machine tools and an electric overhead crane. There were five stabling tracks.

Electrification of the H & CR and the Metropolitan brought several changes to the services operated. The Middle Circle service from Aldgate to Mansion House had been cut back to Earls Court on July 1 1900 and to Kensington Addison Road on January 1 1915, due to congestion on the District tracks east of Earls Court. For the same reason the District Railway, whose trains used the LSWR Richmond line, was not in favour of H & CR trains being extended to Richmond, so the Grove Road Junction was removed in 1916, the signal box there having been closed two years earlier.

In the final years of steam trains to the East London Railway there was a fairly frequent service between Hammersmith and Aldgate, and three trains an hour between Richmond and New Cross (SER). But the East London had not been electrified, so on December 2 1906 the electric service was diverted to Whitechapel District station. Through trains to New Cross were resumed on March 31 1913 after the ELR had been electrified. From December 3 1906 there were four electric trains an hour from Aldgate to Addison Road via the Latimer Road–Uxbridge Road spur, but from October 31 1910 Edgware Road became the terminus for these trains, with the service stepped up to five trains an hour.

In 1908, as is described in an Appendix, 140 acres of exhibition were laid out at what became known as the ''White City'', with a stadium to accomodate the 4th Olympic Games. In anticipation of these events the H & CR decided to open Wood Lane (Exhibition) station in 1908. The contract for this went to Henry Lovatt Ltd for a price of £5,275, but the final cost was £8,516, which included an additional booking office, electric lighting etc; one-third of this amount was paid by Shepherds Bush Improvements Ltd and the Franco-British Exhibition. It was opened on May 1, and Metropolitan posters exhorted the public to ''Book by open-air route'' to the station, which was within the exhibition grounds. The emphasis on open air was presumably to woo passengers away from the Central London Railway, which had its own tube station at White City.

Following the closure of the Franco-British Exhibition on October 31 1908 Wood Lane station was served by alternate trains only. From October 31 1914 Wood Lane closed for regular traffic, re-opened for one day on November 5 1920 for a motor exhibition and afterwards for special events at the White City only. Renamed Wood Lane (White City) in 1920, its title was abbreviated to just White City by London Transport on November 23 1947. Fire damage on October 25 1959 precipitated its final closure on that day.

In December 1910 improvements in the train service between Hammersmith and the City were introduced, with a six-minutes interval between trains instead of the ten-minutes service previously provided. Alternate trains did not call at Wood Lane, Latimer Road and Royal Oak, reducing the journey time from Hammersmith to Moorgate to 25 minutes – more competitive with the District Railway, whose trains took 20 minutes between Hammersmith and Mansion House. However the omission of the stops at Latimer Road and Royal Oak was short-lived, lasting only until February 1911.

On October 4 1909 the H & C Joint Committee accepted an offer from the Metropolitan to supply two old pattern passenger coaches fitted with wire brushes for clearing ice from the conductor rails between Bishops Road, Hammersmith and Addison Road, the cost of £200 to be shared between the Metropolitan and GWR. These vehicles were probably two Met ''rigid-eight'' coaches made redundant by electrification.

On November 23 1911 a contract for a power signalbox at Latimer Road with track circuiting and semi-automatic signalling was given to McKenzie & Holland, at an estimated cost of £1,400. Electric lighting had been installed at Shepherds Bush, Latimer Road and Notting Hill stations in 1907, at a total cost of £835, and a new refreshment

WHITE CITY DAYS . . .

Huge billboard at Finchley Road indicates the importance the Met attached to White City Business.

Quiet time at Wood Lane Station with the Exhibition towers visible behind.

IN THE SEVENTIES . . .

Right: *Diving into the Underpass Tunnel at Westbourne Park on 26 February 1977. C69 Stock forms a Hammersmith– Whitechapel service.*

Below: *A bird's-eye view as a Whitechapel– Hammersmith train enters Royal Oak station on 16 May 1973.*

Photos: Brian Morrison

room, operated by Spiers & Pond, was opened in June 1907 at Hammersmith. On December 17 1922 lock-and-block working was discontinued, signals being controlled by track circuit. Colonel Pringle, who inspected the new arrangements for the Ministry of Transport, agreed that, with the provision of a.c. track circuits to both roads, and five semi-automatic and three automatic signals in place of those formerly mechanically worked, Shepherds Bush signal box could be closed permanently and Ladbroke Grove would be retained for emergency use only. The extension of automatic signalling between Westbourne Park and Bishop's Road, however, had to wait until 1929; the Great Western seemed rather reluctant to agree to it earlier.

Electric traction had presumably not brought all the benefits expected in terms of increased passengers, as on July 31 1911 the Officers Conference of the Met and the GWR recommended that illuminated electric signs reading "Electric Trains every few Minutes to All Parts" should be erected at Hammersmith, Shepherds Bush, Latimer Road, Notting Hill and Westbourne Park stations: on October 16 the tender of the Brilliant Sign Company for supplying these was accepted.

A Stations Commission, chaired by John Wardle, the Metropolitan Commercial Manager, reported in 1914 on Hammersmith & City line stations. Latimer Road had shown an increase of 83,000 passengers in 1913 as compared with five years earlier, mainly due to the opening up of the St Quintin's Park Estate. Shepherds Bush and Goldhawk Road traffic also continued to improve, despite competition from buses, trams and the Central London tube railway. But at Westbourne Park the story was not so happy; here passengers had fallen from 243,352 in 1889 to 162,578 in 1914, once again due to tramway competition. At Hammersmith it was felt that the station suffered from its rather obscure situation, off the main road. To the London United Tramways electric services had been added those of the LCC, who had opened their electric tram routes from Hammersmith to Harlesden in 1908 and to Putney Bridge in 1909. It was suggested that a few fast morning and evening trains between Hammersmith and Bishop's Road would capture a bigger share of the West End and City traffic.

In 1912 improvements were made at Hammersmith station; the existing booking office was converted into shops, with a free-standing booking office in the middle of the concourse, and a new entrance was opened on the Broadway, with a shopping arcade leading into the concourse; these works cost £1,230 in all.

A Metropolitan Railway memorandum stated in 1912 that earnings per mile on the H & CR were only £18,000, compared with £34,000 on the Metropolitan itself (excluding the Harrow and Uxbridge section), and £22,000 on the Great Northern & City Railway. Working expenses were 77.64% of receipts, compared with only 49% on the Met and 49.18% on the G N & City. But soon the Metropolitan managed to get a greater control over its working of the Hammersmith & City; on January 1 1913 an agreement was signed with the GWR which gave the Metropolitan responsibility to maintain and work the H & CR as part of its own undertaking, but on behalf of the H & C Joint Committee. The Great Western was rather reluctant to surrender so much control to the Met but eventually agreed. It was stipulated that the GWR should continue to have full access to its coal yard at Hammersmith and its goods yard at Westbourne Park. Additional capital for improvements felt necessary would be provided by the Metropolitan, with interest on that capital to be paid at 4% of the average net receipts of the line over the years 1909 to 1911. Electric current would continue to be supplied by the Great Western. As a result of this agreement, 14 Great Western staff were transferred to the Metropolitan payroll on January 1 1913.

On January 21 1913 Selbie, the Met general manager, received permission from his board to spend £2,000 on minor improvements at Hammersmith & City stations, including a vertical "Underground" sign over the entrance to the booking office at Latimer Road. It was also decided in 1913 that the existing station at Shepherds Bush, which was midway between Goldhawk Road and Uxbridge Road, should be replaced by a resited Shepherds Bush station and a new station at Goldhawk Road. A tender for these from a local firm, William Brown & Sons (Builders) Ltd, was accepted at a price of £9,569 for the two stations, including 6 months maintenance. Acquisition of property at Goldhawk Road cost £1,337. The new Shepherds Bush station was situated on the north side of the Uxbridge Road, while Goldhawk Road station was on the south side of its namesake. Both stations were opened on April 1 1914, and after one year's operation they could show a net increase of 16.10% in receipts, which represented a net return of 23.10% on the total cost of building them.

This happy state of affairs was not to prevail for very long, however. Bus competition from "General" buses was growing; the very successful "B" type bus had been introduced in 1910 and this was soon followed by improved "K" and "S" types.

The coming of the Great War brought changes to the Hammersmith & City Railway; steps were taken in November 1915 to reduce lighting in stations and trains as an air raid precaution, and as an economy measure in November 1918 the Addison Road to Edgware Road train service was temporarily reduced to one per hour from 6 am to 10 pm, with no Sunday trains, thus saving about 150,000 train miles per annum; this took effect just after Armistice Day, but presumably coal stocks at power stations were still low and savings had to be made.

Another result of the war was the opening of a factory in Brook Green Road, Hammersmith, just north-east of the station yard, by the Ford Motor Co. (England) Ltd. This was used for the assembly of cars for the War Office, which would be despatched by road and rail. A siding, opened in December 1916, with two tracks serving a platform 217ft long, was provided and linked to the H & CR. In December 1919 Ford disposed of these premises to International Motors Ltd, together with part of the siding, which was transferred on February 2, 1920. In October 1923 the premises changed hands again, passing to the French motor firm Citroen, and the siding was assigned to them.

In April 1921 the Metropolitan's accountant prepared a report on the financial position of the Hammersmith & City Railway. He said that until 1900 the line had been reasonably profitable, but after that year it could no longer be considered a successful undertaking; factors were competition from electrified tramways, the opening of the Central London Railway in 1900, and the cost of electrifying the line in 1906. The Great Western felt that further capital expenditure would not produce more revenue and so could not be justified. But the Metropolitan were more optimistic, and under the 1912 agreement they had agreed to spend a sum not exceeding £80,000, of which up to the end of 1920 £16,016 had been expended.

It would appear from this report that the Metropolitan were considering purchasing the Great Western share in the H & CR, and the report sets out in some detail the financial aspects of a possible purchase, which would involve three items, i.e., the Hammersmith & City Railway itself, the Rolling Stock and Car sheds at Hammersmith, and the railway between Westbourne Park and Bishops Road, which connected the H & CR with the Metropolitan system. In the first two items the Met were already joint owners, and the third was solely Great Western property.

The report was probably requested by the Metropolitan and the Great Western directors but no direct action was taken on it. However in 1923 it was agreed that the GWR share of the rolling stock (20 motors and 40 trailers) should be sold to the Metropolitan for £125,000, and that the car sheds at Hammersmith should be leased to the Met with effect from the same date, January 1 1923. The Metropolitan would charge the Joint Committee for working the line at the general cost per mile (a maximum of 5½d excluding the cost of current). Henceforth the Met would supply current, with the existing Park Royal substation fed from Neasden.

Although now fully owned by the Metropolitan, the coaches kept their original livery and lettering "Metropolitan & Great Western Railways" etc., and some trains were still in this style in 1938, five years after London Transport had taken over although by this time the cream upper and fascia panels had been discontinued.

A long memo in June 1925 by the Hammersmith & City Joint Committee to Selbie, the Met General Manger, goes into the question of bus competition in some detail. It contains a reference to government measures to curb this competition, which was heightened by large numbers of independent "pirate" buses which were appearing on the streets. It seems likely that this memo was in reply to a request by Selbie as to the effect of buses on the line's takings; in the previous year the government had introduced the London Traffic Act, which restricted the number of buses which could run along congested streets; the Act, which took effect in 1926, designated 695 streets as "congested". So this legislation may have been behind concern on Selbie's part as to the effect of the buses on the H & CR. The memo states that buses in Central London, which numbered about 3,500 in 1922, had increased to about 5,000 three years later.

It said that a steady decline in short and long distance H & CR traffic had taken place in the post-war period, especially in season tickets, due to the vastly increased facilities offered by the buses, together with further cutting of fares by the "pirate" buses. More general use of "wireless instruments" had affected travel at night in the winter months to visit places of entertainment. Consideration was given to introducing a one-penny fare, but this would be no use unless more frequent trains were put on, and in order to recoup the loss of revenue on a one-penny fare an additional 369,840 passengers per month would be needed. Stations should be provided with better lighting and be more prominently signposted.

In contrast, a problem of a different sort arose in 1928, when the Great Western were pressing George Hally, the Met chief mechanical engineer, to strengthen Hammersmith & City line trains from 6 to 7 or 8 cars. This would prove difficult because the 150hp motor cars could not handle a longer train without having increased power. Purchase of new 275hp motor cars to replace those of 150hp would meet the case, but this would be very expensive. Alternatives were (a) the incorporation of one redundant 150hp Westinghouse motor from the Inner Circle service, or (b) withdrawal of some 6-car trains and utilisation of their motor cars to provide a third 150hp BTH motor car in some trains.

These considerations were the subject of a memo from Hally to the Met locomotive shops superintendent.

Later it was suggested that the Hammersmith & City should purchase 20 motor cars from the Metropolitan, but this was not favoured by the Great Western, who said the only answer to the problem was a more frequent service. The annual cost of *hiring* 20 Metropolitan motor cars would be £7.419. The GWR did not suggest how a more frequent service could be run with the existing number of trains; in dealing with the Metropolitan over H & CR matters one senses a certain lack of co-operation on the part of the GWR, especially if capital expenditure was involved. In the event, the whole question of longer trains was discussed at a meeting of the Great Western & Metropolitan Officers Conference at Baker Street on August 9 1929, when the matter was left in abeyance. However, four Metropolitan 150hp GE76 trains were transferred to the H & CR in 1930, and these may have helped to mitigate the problem.

Reconstruction of the bridges over the West London Railway and Wood Lane, originally postponed to save money, had become urgent by the end of 1931, and the tender of Dorman Long & Co. Ltd at £8,175 was accepted, permanent way work and moving cables bringing the total cost up to an estimated £11,800.

On July 1 1933 the newly-formed London Passenger Transport Board absorbed the Metropolitan Railway, and that company's representatives on the Hammersmith & City Joint Railways Committee were replaced by J. S. Anderson (who had succeeded Selbie as general manager of the Met), J. P. Thomas and C. S. Louch, the latter resigning in March 1934, being replaced by Frank Pick.

In 1935 traffic from the Metropolitan Line to stations between Aldgate and Barking had increased dramatically, causing serious overcrowding in District trains. Traffic to the Barking line was 74% higher than to the East London Line, but no through trains were provided to cater for it, although a through service to New Cross on the ELR had been running for many years. Housing and factory development at Dagenham, Becontree, Upminster etc had given rise to this increase, and passengers between Aldgate and Barking now numbered 30 million per annum. It was therefore decided to run an additional service of trains between Hammersmith (H & C) and Barking at peak hours only, half of the trains previously running to New Cross being diverted to Barking. This service commenced on May 5 1936, using the new "M" Class clerestory stock of basically District Railway design; at the same date First Class accommodation was withdrawn from the Hammersmith & City Line.

On December 19 1935 the LPTB's chief engineer reported that the condition of bridges, permanent way, stations and signalling on the H & C line was much below that of the Board's railways, and a programme was drawn up to provide for the replacement of six bridges and 4½ miles of track in the next five years. This was part of London Transport's New Works Programme 1935–1940, which included extending the tubes over the GWR in the western suburbs and the LNER in Essex. For the H & C it entailed spending £16,000 on permanent way, £6,500 on current rail, £27,900 on bridges and £15,200 on signalling.

In December 1936 an experimental 6-car train of District Railway type was introduced on the Hammersmith & City line with passenger-operated push button doors. Doors could be opened individually at stations, though for safety reasons they were all closed by the guard. Proving successful, this type of train was introduced more widely. The inspection pits on Nos 3 and 4 roads at Hammersmith depot, which were short, were extended in December 1938 to make it possible to inspect 6-car trains; this cost £1,000.

A further change in rolling stock took place in 1937, when new trains with metadyne control, designated "O" stock, were ordered. These differed from previous designs in having side panels which sloped inwards above the waistline and were flared outwards at the bottom, eliminating the use of footboards. The 116 cars of the original order were replacements for the old H & CR joint stock, and ran in 6-car formations. The old trains went into store as their replacements arrived, but in 1942 four LT 6-car trains were lent to the Mersey Railway until 1945, 18 cars out of the 24 being of original H & CR stock.

Douglas Stuckey

Hammersmith bound train crossing the bridge north of Goldhawk Road station with West London traffic chaos below.

Frank Goudie

Metropolitan electric locomotive No 16 "Oliver Goldsmith" on SLS special train at Hammersmith 22 September 1957.

Two spruce trains wait at a quiet and sunlit Hammersmith in the summer of 1998.

ASPECTS OF HAMMERSMITH 1998 . . .

Car sheds seen from the station. The Palais de Dance building lies to the right of the picture.

Station entrance framed by the metal arches advertising the Piccadilly and District station across the Broadway.

Tranquil midday . . .

. . . Philosophical night.

Photos: Douglas Stuckey

A note under the heading "Football Arrangements – Shepherds Bush" in the Working Timetable for November 20 1939 says that on Saturdays when Queen's Park Rangers 1st Team were playing "at home" a 6-car train must be manned in time to work as required to clear return traffic. The District Traffic Superintendent was to arrange this. A similar note appears in the WTT for March 13 1941.

World War II brought considerable war damage during the "Blitz", including damage to the viaduct from Latimer Road to Wood Lane, Hammersmith depot in October 1940 (£4,035), to Wood Lane station (£1,933) in the following month, and many other examples of bomb destruction. Because of the bomb damage the train service between Edgware Road and Kensington Addison Road was withdrawn from 20 October 1940, never to resume.

Despite the war, however, by June 26 1942 repairs to the permanent way and current rails had been completed, costing less than estimated, and four bridges had been rebuilt. The signalling work scheduled under the New Works Programme, however, had been postponed.

The Citroen sidings at Hammersmith were now occupied by the Osram GEC Lamp Works, who were working for the Air Ministry on war production, which required a continuous supply of hydrogen. This was delivered by rail, and necessitated providing a short loop on which wagons could stand while hydrogen gas was withdrawn from them by high pressure pipeline. The Air Ministry agreed to pay the cost of this loop line, estimated at £120, plus a nominal land rent. The work was approved in June 1943, and a year later improved lighting at the Citroen sidings was needed to enable working in the black-out: once again the cost (£110) was met by the Air Ministry.

On December 15 1945 the replacement of the yard lighting at Hammersmith with modern concrete poles and floodlighting was authorised at an estimated cost of £540. On the same date the Southern Railway requested that Bridge HC23 at Goldhawk Road (the bridge which carried the H & C over the now closed SR Shepherds Bush line) should be repaired after war damage; this was Southern Railway property and they would meet the cost of these repairs, expected to amount to £8,350. In December 1946 the installation of a carriage-washing plant at Hammersmith depot was authorised.

A further change in status for the Hammersmith & City Railway came on January 1, 1948, when the two partner companies were nationalised. The GWR became the Western Region of the Railway Executive, and the LPTB became the London Transport Executive. For purposes of management and control the Hammersmith & City Line was incorporated in the LTE, with the exception of Westbourne Park station. The electrified tracks between the latter station and Paddington Suburban were handed over to the LTE on January 1 1970.

The rebuilding of the two bridges over Portobello Road and St Mark's Road near Ladbroke Grove station, whose reconstruction under the New Works programme had been postponed, was carried out in June 1947 by J. Westwood & Co. Ltd; theirs was the lowest tender, but still cost £18,299, well over the original estimate, and work carried out by the Board itself cost a further £5,178 – such was the rise in prices due to the war. On November 23 1947 Wood Lane station was renamed "White City".

The only goods yard on the Hammersmith & City was at Hammersmith, and was Great Western property. It consisted of two sidings on the west side of the station, from the westernmost of which wagon turntables gave access to two sidings for general merchandise and one for the coal depot, at which Rickett Cockerill had a wharf. Coal was the chief commodity handled; the LPTB working timetable for November 20

1939 showing a GWR coal train leaving Old Oak Common at 1.38 am, arriving at Hammersmith at 1.50 am. This working left Hammersmith with empties at 3.20 am for Latimer Road, where it reversed and ran to Addison Road, arriving at 3.52 am, where the empties were presumably berthed. There were three coal trains a week on this basis, but following the 1940 bombing the working timetable for March 3 1941 leaves the timings blank, and states that a Special Notice would be issued showing the times at which these trains would operate. The goods and coal trains ceased in 1960, the traffic having presumably been lost to road transport.

At the time of writing, services are provided with "C69" stock, introduced in 1970, made up in two-car units formed of a motor car and a trailer, and usually marshalled in 6-car trains. There are four pairs of sliding doors on each side of the cars; they have aluminium-alloy bodies which were originally unpainted, but the trains have recently been refurbished and painted in an attractive cream, red and blue colour scheme. Interior finish has also been upgraded, and a public address system is included, over which the name of the next station is announced. "C77" stock, virtually identical with "C69" cars, is also employed on Hammersmith & City services. There are trains to and from Barking at approximately 8 minute intervals at peak hours and during the day on Mondays to Fridays; on Saturdays and Sundays the service interval is 10 minutes until 10 am and after 9 pm.

It would be idle to pretend that a journey on the Hammersmith & City line is a very exciting experience; the line is mostly on viaduct; the stations, which are very close together, are rather nondescript, with the exception of Ladbroke Grove. This was built in 1902 at a cost of £13,836, and is a substantial building in red brick with stone window stills and facings; the steel and glass platforms canopies are not supported on pillars but are cantilevered out from the station walls. It was renamed Ladbroke Grove (North Kensington) in 1919 but became plain Ladbroke Grove again in 1938.

Apart from electrification and the closure of the former LSWR line from Addison Road and Shepherds Bush, the Hammersmith & City Railway has changed very little over the years, however much its clientele may have marched with the times.

WORKING OF COAL TRAINS TO AND FROM HAMMERSMITH YARD.

The 1.10 a.m. Old Oak Common to Hammersmith (Target No. 2) may be made up to 35 wagons (exclusive of two brake vans which must be attached) and work at the times shewn in Nos. 1 and 2 Service Time Tables.

Must run via Up Goods Line from Old Oak Common East to Ladbroke Grove and cross there to the Up Carriage Line and run to No. 1 Carriage Line. Engine to run round train in No. 1 Carriage Line and depart for Hammersmith via Down Main Line and Crystal Palace Loop.

The return train 3.20 a.m. Hammersmith to Old Oak Common runs via Kensington as shewn in Nos. 2 and 17 Service Time Tabes, but if it is not able to leave there before 4.30 a.m. the load must not exceed 20 ordinary 10-ton wagons and 2 goods brake vans.

On the return journey from Hammersmith the whole of the train must be drawn clear of the crossover road in Latimer Road station, the engine then cut off and run to Westbourne Park to return on the westbound line. The engine will then back through the crossover road and take the train to Kensington (Olympia) on the right road.

Whilst the train is standing on the eastbound line, the Signalman at Latimer Road must place lever collars on the eastbound main and eastbound branch line home signals.

It is important that this train works punctually to and from Hammersmith.

See page 34 for emergency working from Old Oak Common via North Pole Junction and Kensington (Olympia).

East to West Through Hammersmith – South Western, District & Piccadilly

The Metropolitan District Railway was conceived as part of a scheme to make an inner circle of railways north of the Thames. The Metropolitan Railway, the northern half of this, was authorised to build the sections from Paddington to South Kensington in the west, and to Aldgate and Tower Hill in the east; their line was opened from Bishops Road, Paddington to Farringdon Street on January 10 1863, the first underground railway in the world, and by December 1868 it had been extended to South Kensington. Powers for the companion scheme, the Metropolitan District, to complete the circle of lines between South Kensington and Tower Hill and branches from South Kensington to the West London line at Addison Road and West Brompton were granted by an Act of July 29 1864. This was a separate company, but the District Board included four directors from the Metropolitan. It was generally expected that the two companies would amalgamate when the Inner Circle was completed.

The contract for the first section, from South Kensington to Westminster Bridge ("Westminster" from 1907) was awarded to a consortium headed by Peto & Betts, and it was opened on December 24 1868, the date on which the Metropolitan had reached South Kensington. The District was worked from the outset by the Metropolitan, using Beyer Peacock 4-4-0 tank engines and "rigid-eight" non-bogie coaches, the service was regulated by a joint committee, the Metropolitan paying the District 55% of the gross receipts on local traffic and a proportion of the through traffic which developed later. Strenuous efforts had been made to get the District line from South Kensington to Westminster ready for the Christmas traffic, and with the employment of 3,000 men this was achieved by Christmas Eve.

A further section of the District Railway was opened, one mile in length, from Gloucester Road to West Brompton on April 12 1869, worked initially as a shuttle service. It had been intended to make a connection with the West London Extension Railway at West Brompton so that trains of the LB & SCR and the LSWR could run over the District by this route, but the connection was never made, and District trains terminated at a separate station adjoining the WLER platforms on the east side.

Through trains did not commence running to West Brompton until August 1 1870, two months after the extension to Blackfriars was opened; this service, like all those of the District Railway at this time, was worked by the Metropolitan.

All these sections of the District Railway were built by the "cut and cover" method, where a wide trench was excavated to take the rails and then lined with side walls and covered with brick arching or girders so that the surface could be restored. This caused some disruption to street traffic during construction, and to minimise expensive acquisition of property along the route the course of the line ran below streets and thoroughfares wherever possible. A pedestrian subway to the Houses of Parliament was opened at Westminster Bridge and brought into use on February 8 1870; the body of William Ewart Gladstone was conveyed through this subway on May 25 1898, when it was brought by rail from Hawarden to lie in state in Westminster Hall. Work was begun on the extension from Westminster Bridge to Blackfriars on August 9 1869; the tracks were laid along the newly built Thames Embankment, which had been opened to pedestrians on July 30 1868. The work could have been combined with the construction of the Embankment itself, but Sir John Fowler, the District's Engineer, decided it would be safer to wait until the Embankment was finished and waterproof. The line to Blackfriars was opened on May 30 1870, a remarkably short time, and seven weeks before, the Embankment, now named the Victoria Embankment, was opened by the Prince of Wales.

The independent directors of the District Railway had become dissatisfied with the working of their railway by the Metropolitan, and gave notice of their intention to terminate the working agreement on July 3 1871. The Metropolitan directors resigned, and the District appointed as its Managing Director James Staats Forbes, General Manager and later Chairman of the London Chatham & Dover Railway. This appointment had far-reaching implications, and raised the curtain on a long period of acrimonious relations with the Metropolitan, whose Chairman from 1872, Sir Edward Watkin, had for years been a bitter opponent of Forbes. The antagonism and rivalry which had obtained between the LCDR and the South Eastern Railway, whose respective leaders Forbes and Watkin also were, was carried over into dealings between the District and the Metropolitan, a state of affairs which was disastrous between two companies who should have been amicable partners. It delayed for years the completion of the Inner Circle, and when that was eventually completed the two companies went to the lengths of having separate booking offices at those stations which were jointly owned.

Meantime elsewhere the London & South Western Railway had opened from Clapham Junction to Richmond, via Wandsworth and Putney in 1846, and this line was extended to Windsor three years later.

From 1860 North London Railway trains were able to reach Richmond via the LNWR, the Hampstead Junction Railway and the North & South West Junction Railway to Kew, where they joined the LSWR. Richmond was something of a Mecca for railway promoters at this period; it was the chief riverside town and was becoming a prosperous suburb with a good quota of commuters to the City. In 1869 Kensington was another shining name in London's wealthy firmament and another district offering rich rewards in passenger traffic, even though the main area of building was nearly a mile to the east of Kensington (Addison Road) station (as it had been renamed from simple Kensington in 1868). The LSWR was anxious to open a second route to Richmond, over a new line from just north of Addison Road on the West London Railway to Hammersmith and thence westward. The Bill heard in the House of Commons in March 1864 for the LSWR (Kensington and Richmond Railway) received some searching and not entirely unfair questioning in Committee. Here the Chairman probes the LSWR's solicitor:–

"They (the LSWR) having a line upon the south side of the Thames (in Richmond) do you see any particular reason why we should have a line upon the north side of the

Thames in addition to that used by other companies at the present time. At the present time you come down to Barnes and run along to Richmond.''

"They propose to get to Richmond by going over the West London Extension and making to Richmond on the north side. In your judgement will the public be better served by the SW making that line than it being served by the NSWJR or any other company?''

"... the LSWR being a very large system of lines have more running powers and more locomotives and so on at their disposal than the smaller lines.''

"You think that they having a monopoly it should be extended?''

"If they do their work properly.''

"Do you say there is a lack of trains between Kensington and London now?''

"Yes.''

"Who manages that line, the SW company?''

"I suppose they do.''

"Then that lack is their fault?''

"It is a lack – I suppose they want the passengers.'

"Does it not look as if there is no very great traffic between Kensington and London now?''

Nevertheless the LSWR (K & R Rly) secured its Act and it was brought into use on 1 January 1869.

The London & South Western's line from the West London Railway to Hammersmith (Grove Road) and Richmond has already been mentioned in the section on the Hammersmith & City Railway. Opened on January 1 1869; it left the WLR 24 chains north of Addison Road, curving round in a semi-circular course to the west and then south, passing under the Hammersmith & City line just south of Goldhawk Road, then running parallel with the latter until reaching Hammersmith Grove Road station. This was built on an embankment whose nature necessitated wooden platforms. A contemporary description said it was "sheltered by generous canopies on decorated cast-iron columns''. At street level on the east side was a two-storey station house with round-arched windows, said to be "handsome and commodious''. Just east of the point where the line passed under the Hammersmith & City, the LSWR opened a station called Shepherds Bush in 1874. Beyond Grove Road the LSWR line ran westward on a 20 ft high embankment for just over a mile.

The new railway was extended westwards through Gunnersbury and over the river to Richmond, and the LSWR operated a train service to Waterloo, via Addison Road, the West London and West London Extension Railways.

A junction between the H & CR and the new LSWR line was made to the north of Hammersmith, and was opened on June 1 1870; this permitted Great Western and Metropolitan trains to work through to Richmond over the LSWR.

"The LSWR ran ten trains per day to Ludgate Hill . . . In fact this was an extension of the Ludgate Hill – Kensington service, and was the LSWR's bid to get from Richmond into the City of London. The 14½ mile journey took 65 minutes and has been described by one writer (C. E. Klapper) as follows:

> '. . . as the trains wended their way . . . and changed direction from
> south east to north east, south east again and then east and north,
> it must have seemed desperately roundabout compared with a
> horse bus from Hammersmith to Piccadilly.'' '

The Great Western began a service from Bishops Road, Paddington to Richmond in 1870; this was withdrawn in the same year but reinstated in 1894. In 1877 the Metropolitan began their Aldgate to Richmond service to compete with the newly extended District Railway; like the GWR trains, this was routed via the Hammersmith & City line. Both these services continued until the H & CR was electrified in 1906; the Metropolitan were not interested in running electric trains to Richmond, but until 1910 the GWR provided a service to Richmond, using steam trains running every half hour from Ladbroke Grove.

Meanwhile, the District Railway had appeared on the scene. As we have seen its first section from South Kensington to Westminster Bridge was opened on December 24 1868. It was extended to West Brompton on April 12 1869, worked initially as a shuttle service. On September 9 1874 the District Railway was extended from Earls Court to Hammersmith Broadway (the Hammersmith Extension Railway, leased to the District for 999 years). A short further extension took District railway metals to Studland Road Junction and the LSWR, giving District trains access to Richmond. This short link was opened in 1877 and the District commenced a service from Richmond to the Mansion House. Electrification of the LSWR from Richmond to Turnham Green and of the District from Turnham Green to Whitechapel was brought about on August 1 1905.

A further extension from Turnham Green to Ealing Broadway was opened on July 1 1879. It was hoped to extend even further to Uxbridge, but this was opposed by the Great Western. The latter relented later to the extent of allowing the District to operate a service from Mansion House through Ealing to Windsor. This was not a success, however, and lasted only from March 1 1883 to September 30 1885, Still further extensions were from West Brompton to Putney Bridge, opened on March 1 1880, from Mill Hill Park (now Acton Town) to Hounslow Town, opened on May 1 1883, and from Osterley to Hounslow Barracks (now Hounslow West) on July 21 1884. The old Hounslow Town station was replaced on March 31 1886 by a new station at Heston Hounslow (renamed Hounslow Central in 1925).

Whatever the limitations of the K & R one of the happier results of its opening was the development in 1875–81 of the first garden suburb, Bedford Park, served by the station at Turnham Green whose station name boards continue to carry the 'For Bedford Park' inscription today. This leafy estate was largely the work of the architect, Norman Shaw, and became famous as an 'arty' community:

> "There was a village builded
> For all who are aesthete,
> Whose precious souls it fill did,
> With utter joy complete."

One of the many causes of friction between the LSWR and District was the height of the platforms; the LSWR built their platforms only 1ft 9ins above rail level, whilst the District trains were designed for platforms 3ft 1ins. This difference was a peril to travellers, particularly the voluminously skirted women of the time and, after a number of accidents, pressure from the Board of Trade forced action, the LSWR raising their platforms to conform with the higher level universal on British railways.

"In 1901 the common section of 70 chains between Studland Road Junction and Turnham Green saw eighteen westbound trains between 5.00 pm and 7.00 pm

A VARIETY OF STATIONS

Top: *Shepherds Bush LSWR.*
Middle: *The Piccadilly station and signal box at Hammersmith before opening, 1906.*
Bottom: *Barons Court.*

London Transport Museum

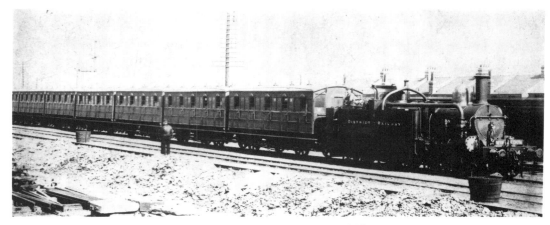

Early District Railway stock and steam locomotive 4-4-0T No 4 in 1905.

Train from Southend hauled by two District electric locomotives at Hammersmith in early 1930's.

'All Stations' Ealing-bound train of E-type stock at Turnham Green 1916.

Photos: London Transport Museum

– three LSWR, two Metropolitan and thirteen District, of which four ran to Richmond".* The District foresaw that with forthcoming electrification their train services would increase substantially over this section, and, after some resistance from the LSWR a new rental agreement was signed by the parties on 23 July 1903 allowing the MDR to run as many trains as it wished as long as they did not impede the LSWR and Met/GWR traffic. "Electric traction between Studland Road and Turnham Green commenced with the District's Ealing service on 1 July 1905 and on the Richmond line exactly a month later. Now the two hours of the evening peak saw 30 westbound passenger trains – four LSWR, four GWR (replacing the Met) and 22 District . . .".

1 July 1905, the opening day for the District's electrification in West London brought some embarrassment and red faces. As O. S. Nock noted, the "Railway Magazine" reported these problems at length (and with a hint of relish?) including in part: "The cause of the delay was the flooding of the line at Hammersmith and the junction between West Kensington and Earls Court by most torrential rain. The water, owing to the absence of sufficient drainage, accumulated in such quantities as to entirely flood the rails. An earth connection was formed and the whole of the electric current was diverted.

. . . On some portions of the line out West steam trains found themselves sandwiched between the stationary electric trains. It was impossible to move them also and the consequence was that between nine and ten o'clock the booking offices were closed and passengers were informed that the issue of tickets was temporarily discontinued".

A tank locomotive, a 4-4-0 almost identical to the Beyer Peacocks introduced by the Met, was adopted by the District Railway as its one and only design for steam haulage in its early days. With the advent of electrification the District desired to be done with steam as quickly as possible but there were services such as the LNWR Outer Circle through to Mansion House and later the through Ealing–Southend trains which still needed locomotive haulage. Consequently the MDR acquired 10 Bo Bo electric locomotives each with four 200hp BTH motors, of rather undistinguished design, looking like ancient gypsy caravans and having the clerestory roofs which could be seen on most District stock. The first District multiple units, B Stock, were wooden-bodied and handsome, but chauvinist feathers were ruffled not only by the perhaps inevitably American- influenced styling† but by the fact that two thirds of the 420 cars were to be built in France!

The District was innovator in signalling as in much else; the illuminated track diagram which was installed in 1905 at what was then titled potentially misleadingly Mill Hill Park (now Acton Town) was the precursor of the train control diagrams which were adopted universally afterwards, and these diagrams coupled with track circuiting and automatic electro-pneumatic signalling put the MDR in the position of world leader in this aspect of railway operation.

Written agreements did not meet the pressures of more and more District trains – by 1909 only more track could solve the problem, and a complicated LSWR Bill gave, most importantly, authority for a new set of non-electrified lines for LSWR, and Met and GWR, with the existing southern pair devoted almost exclusively to the District's needs. A new single island platform District station was opened at Stamford Brook on Goldhawk Road on February 1912.

---

*"L & SWR in the Twentieth Century", J. N. Faulkner and R. A. Williams (David & Charles 1988)
†When the Metropolitan District Electric Traction Co Ltd was formed in 1901, the entire capital was owned by 16 American firms or individuals.

The District cometh. Site of new station Hammersmith 1874 . . .

. . . and the opposition fighteth back. Huge billboard for the Hammersmith and City dominates 1901 Broadway. *Photos:* Hammersmith and Fulham Archives

Entrance to Hammersmith (District and Piccadilly lines) station built to a design of Mirale, Tattersfield and Partners and opened 1993.

Sunlight and shadows on eastbound Piccadilly line train under a filigree of metalwork at Hammersmith.

Entrance to Stamford Brook station.

The original MDR station at Hammersmith fell an early victim to fire and was severely damaged on 20 January 1882, taking eight months to repair. The arrival of the Great Northern, Piccadilly and Brompton (later abbreviated to Piccadilly) on 15 December 1906 necessitated a further substantial rebuild with new terminal island platforms for the GNP & B to the north of the existing District provision, and rearranged separate street entrances. The extension of the Piccadilly to South Harrow was inaugurated on July 4 1932 and a new station at Hammersmith in the style of Holden was constructed over the years 1930–33. At the same time the opportunity was taken to build a pedestrian underpass beneath the Broadway, during which work LCC trams crossed it on an horrendously dangerous looking temporary exposed rail structure.

Meanwhile the LSWR steam trains serving Hammersmith declined steadily as passengers forsook them for electric trams and District trains and they were withdrawn as a wartime economy measure on June 5 1916, never to be restored. At one time there were plans for the Central London Railway to be extended to Richmond over the LSWR but it was decided after the war that the Piccadilly would be extended westwards to Hounslow and South Harrow to relieve the District. The northernmost tracks of the four track section between Studland Road Junction and Turnham Green were out of use and the layout was rearranged so that Piccadilly trains would run non-stop between Hammersmith and Action Town on the centre tracks. This required a new platform at Stamford Brook for eastbound District trains and extensive works for them to pass beneath the disused LSWR viaduct at Studland Road

In 1980's a major redevelopment scheme was proposed for the eastern side of the Broadway, including the station area and bus facilities. After long negotiations and many problems, demolition of the existing properties commenced in March 1988, and the Queen Caroline Street entrance was closed from 29 October 1988. Authority for a revised Hammersmith Centre West scheme was finally obtained in January 1989. Closure of the main railway ticket office followed on 10 December 1989 and a temporary office was established further east. The west side high level passageway was also closed and the sole entrance remaining on Hammersmith Broadway brought passengers to the east side of the central station footbridge; an ample area was left for ticket issue and staff-manned barrier inspection. Storm damage precipitated the shutting of the Talgarth Road ticket office on 25 January 1990, four days earlier than intended.

In 1993, as part of the Hammersmith Centre West plan, a new Underground Station built to the designs of Mirale, Tattersfield and Partners was opened below an enclosed island site bus station. It seems a commendable achievement that, deep in the often polluted drear of the Broadway, the architects have managed with glass canopies suspended from side to side lattice steel beams to create a seemingly airy, light construction of white and grey. The original ceramic entablature carrying the old names of the two railways has been incorporated in the building at the top of a long wall facing a large curved window.

The Piccadilly tube started as two separate projects – the Brompton and Piccadilly Circus Railway formed in 1897 to build a 2 mile line as far as South Kensington, and in 1899 came the separate Great Northern and Strand Railway Co., designed to build a tube from Wood Green to Kings Cross and thence beneath the new Kingsway to the Strand. In 1901 the rumbustious American, C. T. Yerkes, purchased both components and amalgamated them as the Great Northern, Piccadilly and Brompton Railway with powers to link the two lines between Holborn and Piccadilly Circus. During 1902–3 the

GNPBR was extended westward in company with the MDR, rising to the surface just east of Barons Court station and terminating at the northern platform of Hammersmith. A car depot and works was established at Lillie Bridge, which depot had been left by the MDR which moved its base to Ealing Common in 1905. The new route to Hammersmith was opened by Lloyd George, then President of the Board of Trade, on 15 December 1906.

Birds Eye View of Hammersmith (Holden Station) in 1933 with eastbound Piccadilly train and LCC tramcar.

Photo: London Transport Museum

ENGINE-ROOM OF POWER-HOUSE, WHERE ELECTRICITY IS GENERATED BY SIX ENGINES OF 1,200 H.P. EACH

The switchboard from which the current is controlled will be seen at the far end of the engine-room on a gallery commanding a view of the room

TWO FIFTY-FIVE TON ELECTRIC LOCOMOTIVES IN SHEDS

These have now been displaced by the motor car trains. The steam locomotive used about the yard is also shown

VIEW OF POWER-HOUSE FROM CAR SHEDS

A train may be seen being drawn out by a steam locomotive on to the current rail

REAR END OF TRAIN STARTING FOR ENTRANCE TO TUNNEL

All the photographs on this page were specially taken for "The Tatler" by Campbell and Gray

Behind the scenes at the Twopenny Tube.

Central London

The Central London Railway had distinguished beginnings. It was opened by the Prince of Wales on 27 June 1900 and among those concerned with the companies promoting the enterprise were many of the Prince's intimates – Sir Ernest Cassel, Lord Colville, Sir Francis Knollys (private secretary to Edward), and there was a cosmopolitan flavour to the principal shareholders who included Frenchmen, Germans and Austrians, and Americans of whom Darius Ogden Mills was to be director of both the CLR and General Electric of America (to whom the contract for much of the line's original rolling stock and operational equipment was given). At the inaugural luncheon in the generating station at Wood Lane the American interest was further represented by the perhaps unexpected presence of Samuel Clemens (Mark Twain).

The CL was a deep-level electric tube planned to link the City (firstly from a terminus at the Bank) and that traffic node of growing importance at Shepherds Bush, following the east to west highway under Holborn, Oxford Street and Bayswater Road which together formed one of the busiest city thoroughfares of the expanding European world. The traffic available was ripe for development but this had been inhibited by a Royal Commission of 1846 which had sought to deter railways from building within a Central London area, bounded on the south by the Thames and on the north by what are now the Marylebone, Euston and Pentonville Roads.

The original engineers were Sir John Fowler of Metropolitan Railway fame, Sir Benjamin Baker (Forth Bridge), and J. H. Greathead who had developed and given his name to the excavating shield which made tube railways possible. The first stock issue for the CLR was poorly subscribed, and persuasive words in friendly ears were needed from the powerful big names to get the project financed. All sorts of interested parties kept eagle eyes on the building of the CLR, as it ran through streets, which if not paved with gold, were of vast commercial value. To stay within street limits several stations, including Notting Hill Gate, had the up and down tubes and platforms vertically above one another. For the whole of the electric generating plant, equipment and locomotives the Consulting Engineer was an American, Dr Horace Field Parshall. The generating station and first rolling stock depot were on a 24 acre site at Shepherds Bush, where until then had stood a fine house and garden known as Woodhouse Park: the site was east of Wood Lane and just west of sidings of the West London Railway. The Hammersmith and City line curved across to the north and beyond the H & C lay a still largely underdeveloped area of farms and brickfields, and the many acres of the open spaces of Wormwood Scrubs. Shepherds Bush station was constructed on the north side of Uxbridge Road, at the eastern point of the Common, and a few yards west of Uxbridge Road WLR station. The station was designed by Harry Measures, the chief architect of the CLR. Access to the platforms was initially by three electric lifts but, so heavy was the demand by passengers, that four additional lifts in two additional lift shafts had to be provided as early as 1902/3. In 1914 escalators replaced the lifts and an enlarged ticket hall was completed at the same time.

From the west end of Shepherds Bush station the depot was reached by a single line extension from the westward running line turning sharply north over the constricting

"Caxton curve" and ending in a siding reaching nearly to the roadway of Wood Lane. All traffic entering or leaving the depot had to reverse here, and a long loop line running around the main depot buildings to the eastern side gave a link to the West London Railway, the route for the arrival of coal supplies.

The CLR generating station was a handsome, spacious structure, if not quite as impressive as the LUT generating station not far away at Stamford Brook, and, of course CLR and LUT were destined to become, in due course, co-operative members of the Underground Group. Six 1200 hp generators delivered alternating current at 5500 volts, transformed down at substations to 500 volts dc. At the outset the CLR had third rail operation with the current returning through bonded running rails; it was as late as 1940 that the CLR was converted to four rail operation to match the system on the other tubes and enabling a flexible use of London Transport's rolling stock.

The first CLR trains were gate-ended hauled by lumbering camel-backed electric locomotives built by GE of America, and weighing 43 tons each with direct drive (armatures on axles), these engines battered the rails and caused serious vibration, as well as needing time to change ends at termini, making a short interval time-table impossible. By 1903 the CLR had had to make a dramatic alteration in policy and to replace the destructive locomotives with the first multiple-unit trains, which henceforward became universal on London's tubes.

The cars were purple-brown below waistband and white above with gold lining. The title 'Central London' appeared in 4 inch gold block letters on the panels together with the coat-of-arms, the CLR being one of only two tube companies to have an armorial device. Two condensing oil-fired 0-6-0 steam locos built by Hunslet were normally on duty at Wood Lane, but their curved roof-cabs gave them sufficient clearance for them to haul stock through the tunnels.

To overcome the perceived danger, only the entrance road and line to the electric locomotive shed at Wood Lane depot initially had electrified track. At the end of 1900 electrified trolley wires were erected to cover most of the depot layout, and two locomotives were equipped with trolley poles to shunt within its confines. The overhead wires were not finally abandoned until 1908, by which time the depot had been completely laid with electric track.

With the loss of the bulk of the electric locomotives the loco running shed was reduced in size and, concurrently, a new set of sheds ('Wood Lane Sheds') was constructed to the west of the depot, alongside Wood Lane itself; a fan of lines connected these sheds to the loop line ('South Road') at the back of the original depot buildings.

The inaugural luncheon had been held in a marquee after the Prince of Wales had travelled to Shepherds Bush from the Bank arriving at 3.45 pm, after a journey taking 18 minutes for the 5¼ miles. At the Prince's own desire only one speech was made, his own, and that remarkable for its brevity in those days of oratorical outpourings; "My Lords and gentlemen, I have great pleasure in declaring the CLR open. It has given me much pleasure to take part in today's proceedings. I wish to drink 'Success to the undertaking', and I congratulate Sir Benjamin Baker, the eminent engineer who has constructed this great railway. I have little doubt that it will be an immense boon to London, and I am sure you will all join with me in wishing success to the company." Full public service did not begin until Monday 20 July 1900.

After some debate and a variety of proposals it was agreed that the CLR should have one-class trains and one universal fare of 2d irrespective of distance. This led inevitably to the CLR being christened the "Twopenny Tube". Gilbert was even inspired to change some words in "Patience" to say; "the very delectable, highly respectable, Twopenny Tube young man", instead of "threepenny bus young man". Nevertheless the much derided 'bus in its new motorised guise became a very real competitor and threat to the CLR. This coupled with the electrification of the Inner Circle resulted in a significant fall in numbers of passengers carried.

Meantime, although the problems with its first heavy and damaging locos had been dealt with expeditiously, another highly unpopular 'problem' took longer to solve – the CLR's smell. The CLR's own 'Report on 4 Years Working' published in 1905 stated: "Since all these observations" (of air purity) "were made there has been installed at Shepherds Bush a fan, 20 feet in diameter and electrically driven, which every night after the removal of the trains, draws the air out of the tunnels, from one end of the line to the other. Whenever the traffic stops canvas doors in the station passages, except at the Bank, are closed preventing the admission of air, and draws in the fresh supply by the Bank passages. The force of the fan is such that it produces in each tunnel a current of air of an average velocity of 7 miles per hour; and in the distance of six miles, the fan when working for three hours will renew the tunnel air more than three times."

This remarkable fan does not seem to have totally impressed the public. Sir Theodore Martin in evidence before the Royal Commission on London Traffic in February 1904, avowed "For myself, I could not risk my health by travelling upon such a railway as the Central London, with its obnoxious vapour, which I know from meeting it at the stations, and I hear so many complaints, too, many individuals are giving it up . . .".

Complaints continued until 1911 when, at last, an effective and elaborate pressure system injecting 6,000 cu. ft per minute of filtered and ozoned air was installed.

The same year report had summarised the train services: "the service given is a train every two minutes of 30 trains per hour leaving the Bank or Shepherds Bush. This service can be maintained during the two busy hours of the morning from 8 to 10 and the two evening hours from 5 to 7, and this service can be maintained with 27 trains in the tunnels. At other times of the day a service of 3 to 3½ minutes suffices and this can be given by 16 to 19 trains in the tunnels. Each train consists of 7 cars . . . has seating accomodation for 330 passengers".

A welcome if temporary addition to the CLR's traffic came with the building on over 200 acres of land between Uxbridge Road and the Scrubs, of the White City, (sometimes Great White City), an extravagant and vast private venture of the brothers Kiralfy, already known for their association with Olympia and Earls Court. An exhibition centre with 100 acres of gardens, eight massive halls, half a mile of artificial waterways and a stadium (which housed the 1908 Olympic Games), ensured vast popular interest. The first (Franco-British) exhibition was opened by the new Prince and Princess of Wales (later to be George V and Queen Mary) on May 14 1908, and a further royal visit was by King Edward VII and the French President, presumably this time not on the "Twopenny Tube".

The CLR was ready. By an Act of 26 July 1907 a second line was built to the depot from Shepherds Bush through Wood Lane Sheds to the original reversing siding forming a continuous loop on which was constructed Wood Lane station; the station was immediately opposite the exhibition ground entrance and opened simultaneously with the White City itself on 14 May 1908. A further response to changing conditions was the abandonment of the universal two-penny fare. From 1 July 1907 the rate for a distance of 8 stations or more became 3d, counter-balancing 1d stages were introduced on 14 March 1909 and season tickets were instituted on 1 July 1911. Also, from 1911 a parcels

ASPECTS OF
SHEPHERDS BUSH

The single-storeyed 'Twopenny Tube' station in 1908. The photograph has attracted a gathering of the lads including one with fish and chips.

The same scene 90 years later illustrating West London's capacity for clutter.

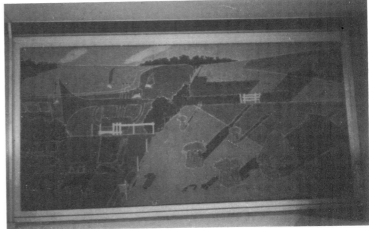

Inside the booking hall Julie King's mural of bucolic symbols has an unlikely rural effect.

Douglas Stuckey

London Transport Museum

White City station in 1999.

Douglas Stuckey

Now a grim façade, a once elegant entrance to Wood Lane station waits for the regeneration long promised for the area.

Douglas Stuckey

service was provided, with parcel sorters on the trains and delivery boys with a fleet of tricycles ready at the stations to whistle their way to final destinations. The Great War had other jobs for "boys" to do and shortage of staff led to the withdrawal of the parcels operation in 1917.

The Underground Electric Railways Co had for some time looked to incorporate the CLR within its Group which already included the Bakerloo, Hampstead and Piccadilly tubes, as well as the District Railway. In 1912 the UER offered to take over the CLR in exchange for new guaranteed stock bearing a dividend of 4%, not perhaps especially enticing, except that the CLR had of recent years been able to provide its shareholders with 3% only. The CLR was absorbed into the UER from 1 Jan 1913.

Although the CLR had not originally envisaged driving out into the outer suburbs, by 1912 it was busy with ambitious ideas for extensions westwards. The "Chiswick Times" Friday 28 June reported "TWOPENNY TUBE EXTENSION, THROUGH RAVENS-COURT PARK TO RICHMOND." An important announcement as to the decision of the Central London Railway to extend their system from Shepherds Bush, through Ravenscourt Park and Kew Gardens to Richmond, was made at the meeting of the Thames Valley Councils Association . . .on Wednesday afternoon . . . it proposed to proceed through Ravenscourt Park, Gunnersbury, Kew Gardens and Richmond to Hampton and Hampton Court. He understood from Dr Parshall that Hampton Court would be the terminal point at present . . . When the delegates complained of the high fares by the LSWR Dr Parshall said that he would be glad to get fares half as high as those now charged." A. H. Stanley, later Lord Ashfield, wrote to the meeting as Managing Director of the District Railway, taking a more circumspect view: "The question of the extension of our line in various districts has the careful consideration of my other directors, but the enormous cost of such extensions, together with the very heavy burden of rates imposed by the authorities, make the cost of such extensions almost, if not quite, prohibitive." (The whirligig of time was later to make Ashfield Managing Director of the Central London himself).

An act of 15 August 1913 authorised a new 2½ mile railway from Shepherds Bush to the LSWR at Gunnersbury, but the Great War put a hold on this and other developments. The cessation on 3 June 1916 of all LSWR Kensington–Richmond passenger services altered the situation, as its tracks between Hammersmith and Turnham Green were now seldom used. Accordingly, in 1920, the CLR and District companies, supported by the LSWR promoted a Bill for two short extensions of the CLR linking their Shepherds Bush station with the LSWR just north of its Hammersmith Grove station. The Underground network was now united under Lord Ashfield who wanted to provide an alternative route from Richmond to the heart of London, but, in the end, plumped for a link from the Piccadilly line to the LSWR instead, although, of course, the Piccadilly never did reach Richmond.

A rather unexpected expansion of the Central London was not initiated by the CLR and was driven by another company's needs and aspirations coming from the west. In 1905 the GWR had secured an Act to build an Ealing and Shepherds Bush Railway to run from the West London north of Uxbridge Road to their Acton and Wycombe line, then under construction, and then south to the main line at Ealing. A short stub branch was to run to a terminus at Shepherds Bush, sited between Providence Place, Sterne Street, Caxton Road and Uxbridge Road, which was to be linked with the CLR by subway. When the CLR built its 1908 extension to Wood Lane it was decided that it would be far more mutually useful to join the GWR and CLR lines north of Wood Lane, allowing through running for CLR trains which obtained running powers over the E & SB to Ealing Broadway. The only GWR passenger trains to use the E & SB were workmen's trains from Greenford to Kensington which ran from 1922 to 1938, being extended to Clapham Junction from 1933.

Wood Lane station's unusual situation on the loop contrived to make it an oddity of construction and operation. In particular, Platform 1, the southern-most platform constricted by a depot turnout was too short for all the doors of a six-coach train, and in March 1928 in an effort to incorporate improved facilities for the passengers for the nearby stadium, a swivelling wooden extension platform, 35 feet long, was provided which could be operated from the signal box to accommodate the sixth carriage. In the beginning Wood Lane had only the two platforms on the loop, but from the opening of the Ealing and Shepherds Bush Railway extension, two additional platforms were provided on the new through tracks.

However, although the GWR was able to commence goods services on 16 April 1917, the Great War caused a long hiatus in the rest of the programme. 22 cars had been built by Brush for the CLR's increased requirements on reaching Ealing but they were diverted in 1917 to complement the Bakerloo's existing stock on its new services to Watford over the LNWR's electrified "New Lines". This stock was transferred back to the CLR when the extension to Ealing finally became operable on 3 August 1920. The only intermediate station on the E & SB on opening was East Acton near the Old Oak housing estate, but others at North Acton and West Acton followed on 5 November 1923. (Acton has Town, Central, North, South, East and West stations which suggests some poverty of imagination and great opportunities for passenger confusion). Power for the Ealing trains was taken from the GWR power station at Park Royal. CLR's Wood Lane power station was reduced to a sub-station only on March 18 1928 and henceforward the CLR drew its current from the Underground's massive station at Lots Road, Chelsea.

In March 1926, the Underground began a complete overhaul and conversion programme for the CLR stock. On the 1903 stock the gated platforms were enclosed and bulkheads removed, and two 3' 6'' openings with single sliding doors were provided on the side of each. Piccadilly stock temporarily adjusted for three-rail running and with smaller trailer wheels to cope with the CLR's more restricted tunnels was transferred for a year to provide a temporary service.

In the 1930's at the time of the provision of a fourth electric rail steps were taken to provide the realignment and additional clearances also needed to allow standard tube stock to operate on the CLR. In the quiet of the nights, over a period of two years, a works train behind a Wood Lane battery locomotive moved through the tunnels removing tunnel segments and taking them back to the depot where they were ground and relined as necessary to achieve the required diameter. In all, 10,000 segments needed alteration. Station tunnels were also lengthened to take eight car trains and at Shepherds Bush, where the exit stairs and escalators at the western end and converging lines towards the east impeded extension, the tracks widened and the platform extended between them as an island. The main tunnelling work was completed by September 1938 but the station alterations took longer and commencement of four-rail operation did not take place until April 1940.

The CLR was absorbed by the London Passenger Transport Board in July 1933 – for a short while it was restyled the Central London Line but from 23 August 1937 this was abbreviated to Central Line. Under the New Works programme of 1935–40, produced by London Transport in conjunction with the LNER and GWR, the GWR agreed, authorised by the GWR (Ealing and Shepherds Bush Railway Extension) Act 1936, to build additional tracks alongside the existing pair from North Acton to Ruislip and Denham for a further substantial extension of CL services. However, it had long been realised that the two tracks originally provided between Shepherds Bush and North Acton would not cope with both GWR goods trains and the growing demands of the CL. Between 1936 and 1938 this section was quadrupled with one pair of tracks reserved exclusively for the electric trains. The Hitler War, which was in so many ways a hideous reprise of 1914–18, once again halted transport plans, and the rails which had been laid beyond North Acton were lifted, being relaid after the War, allowing CL trains to start operating out as far as Greenford on 30 June 1947. The clerestory roof 1923–4 stock which had been cascaded down from the Northern and Bakerloo lines for CL use had mostly been stored in the open during the War pending completion of the Ruislip and other extensions, and required considerable attention at Acton Works, to repair the ravages of weather. Virtually simultaneously a new White City station with two long, approximately 450 foot island platforms and three tracks was built closer to the Stadium, which continued as a sports venue after the exhibition areas had been abandoned to other purposes. Wood Lane station closed on 22 November 1947 and White City opened on the following day.

The White City station was "designed by Kenneth Seymour and A. D. McGill . . . a yellow brick structure in the Holden tradition . . . The two island platforms are served by three roads, the easternmost serving westbound trains – an unusual feature of this station. Other features of interest include a now disused secondary exit opposite the ticket office which served White City stadium traffic, original 1940's lamp standards at the end of each platform and a plaque on the main elevation marking the station's achievement of a Festival of Britain Architecture Award in 1951" to quote from an LT handout prepared for Heritage Day tours of the Central buildings and layout in the area.

From January 1948 management and control of the GWR-owned White City to Ealing Broadway route (excluding the important Ealing Broadway station), and the electrified lines from North Acton Junction to Greenford passed to London Transport. The last extension westwards of the CL was from Greenford to West Ruislip, opened on 21 November 1948, and these electrified lines finally were transferred to London Transport on 1 January 1963. The original intention to press on to Denham had been abandoned.

In 1957 prototype trains from different builders underwent trial on the Piccadilly line but when a large order was placed with Metro Cammell which commenced delivery in 1959 it was decided that the CL's needs were more urgent than those of the Piccadilly and 57 trains were diverted temporarily to the CL where they remained until 1964. A new order for the CL for almost identical stock provided 352 driving motor cars and 118 non-driving motor cars from Metro-Cammell as well as 176 trailers from BR at Derby.

In 1988 approval was given for a £720 million modernisation programme for the CL. 340 2 car emu sets were ordered from BREL and these were equipped with dot matrix screen route destination indicators and closed circuit television platform monitors in the drivers' cabs. At the same time the power supply was increased. In 1991 Pilkingtons were given a contract for a fibre optic infrastructure to link all sites and stations to a central control room.

Shepherd's Bush station was the subject of a substantial "make-over" in the years 1983–5, including the commissioning of a large mural by Julie King of cows, meadows, hayricks and other bucolic items, with its hints of town-life not immediately apparent, and perhaps altogether a somewhat oddly-conceived interpretation of Shepherds Bush's name and origins. Despite this, and the dark green glossy platform tiles with their red diamond borders and other changes, the hall remains a one-storey building with skylights, and from the outside it is initially virtually indistinguishable from early photographs when LUT trams dominated the foreground. Alongside the station a long covered footbridge designed to resemble a BR125 train crosses one end of the Green, although its glories have been sorely diminished by the pollution from the maelstrom of traffic below. The nameplates carry the names of once leading colleagues of Ken Livingstone in ''Fare's Fair'' days.

At the beginning of the Hitler War, in the quiet days before the mortal storm the public was forbidden to use tube stations as Air Raid shelters. But with the commencement of the Blitz authority undertook a swift 'volte-face' and disciplined arrangements were made so that Londoners could take shelter on the platforms whilst still allowing adequate space for travelling passengers. At platform level people were below access to services for sanitation, food preparation etc. The Central Line was chosen for the first tests of facilities for feeding the shelterers – initially at Holland Park electric boilers heated water to provide tea at a penny a cup, and sandwiches were delivered in dust proof containers. The experiment was successful and more than popular, and

Douglas Stuckey

Flat representations of the HST125 lie on either side of the footbridge spanning Shepherds Bush traffic close to the Central line station.

Shepherds Bush was the second station to enjoy the "luxury". By November 1940 refreshments were being provided at nine stations on the Central.

Maeve Binchey has given Shepherds Bush station some literary distinction in her book of stories: "Victoria Line, Central Line" (originally published by Quartet Books in 1978). In the story entitled Shepherd's Bush: "people looked very weary, May thought, and shabbier than she remembered Londoners to be . . . This was Shepherd's Bush where people lived. They had probably set out from here early this morning and fought similar crowds on their way to work. The women must have done their shopping in their lunch-hour because most of them were carrying plastic bags of food. It was London different to the one the tourist sees."

It may not be the most serious of pollutions but one wonders how hungover commuters on Central Line trains today can tolerate the shrill note which precedes the opening and closing of any door whether inflicted by the guard or by individual passengers.

The West London Railway

In 1836 a railway with a title almost longer than its route mileage, the Birmingham, Bristol and Thames Junction Railway, was authorised as a branch three miles long from the London and Birmingham Railway at Willesden to a terminal at the basin of the Kensington Canal (near Hammersmith Road, then called Great Western Road), which had opened in 1828 from the Thames at Chelsea. Bristol had been included in the title because it had been hoped to receive much of the GWR's traffic from that City, but in 1837 the GWR had secured its independent London terminus at Paddington, obviating any need to use another company's line. On 23 July 1840 the BBTJR changed its grandiose name to the brief but much more appropriate West London Railway, but it still had little substantial potential traffic as the LBR itself had easy access to the Regent's Canal at Camden Town, and other outlets, from its own line without recourse to the WLR. Consequently capital was slow in materialising, and the line was not opened until 27 May 1844.

It was built as a single track, with hopes of goods traffic for Kensington and those parts of the Thames near the Canal. Leaving the LBR line near the present Willesden Junction station, it passed to the west of Kensal Green Cemetery and under the Paddington Canal, and crossed the Great Western main line on the level. Proceeding south near Wormwood Scrubs it continued to the canal basin, about ¼ mile south of Kensington High Street. It subsequently had stations at Willesden, at St Quintin Park and Wormwood Scrubs, at Uxbridge Road and a terminus at Kensington. Over the years there have been in fact, three different stations at Kensington; the first, built in 1840 was situated south of the Hammersmith Road near the canal basin and adjoined what later became the Warwick Road goods station of the GWR. The second station was built to secure a more convenient site, and was opened north of the road in 1844; it was described by G. P. Neale, the Superintendent of the LNWR as "the somewhat rough terminus at Kensington High Street". His evident dissatisfaction and the opening of the West London Extension Railway led to the construction of the third, and present, station, opened in 1863 and later named Addison Road. This important station merits more detailed description, because down through the years it has seen a wide spectrum of most types of trains, local and long distance, passenger and freight, steam, electric and diesel-powered, in war and peace. The long main platforms as finally built were 1,100 ft long; only the eastern part was constructed at first, and the long through platform line had a "scissors crossing" halfway along it, so that two trains could use it at once, to get in from or go out to the main through line. On the down side a similar pair of tracks had a similar double crossover, though later one link, down main to down platform, was removed. Terminal bays on the east side had two platforms and three lines, the centre one of which was an engine escape road. All the through lines, and those of the Northeast bay, were laid with mixed gauge track, but the Southeast bay had standard gauge only.

The station building was wood-faced with weather-boarding, and incorporated a booking office, waiting rooms, parcels office and a refreshment room. A ridge-and-furrow type canopy covered the central part of the through platform and the ends of the buildings, with the bay platforms left open. The east side of the station was ready in 1864 and came into use on July 1; the more convenient and capacious layout being immediately found very advantageous. In 1868 it had the suffix "Addison Road" added to its title after the nearby thoroughfare commemorating Joseph Addison, the eighteenth century poet, essayist and statesman. It was renamed Kensington (Olympia) in December 1946.

In 1860 the level crossing away to the north over the Great Western Railway main line was replaced by a bridge, a connection with the GWR was made at North Pole Junction, and with the Hampstead Junction Railway at Willesden. In 1839 the firm of Clegg & Samuda proposed to the West London Railway that they should at their own expense, lay an experimental atmospheric railway from Uxbridge Road to the London & Birmingham line. The system to be used had been patented by Henry Pinkus, using the pressure of air on a piston fitted under the train, which ran in a pipe from which the air ahead of it had been withdrawn by pumping, thus creating a vacuum which propelled the train. Pinkus had built a machine to run on a short stretch of pipe and rails beside the Kensington Canal. But when the West London Railway took over the Canal they cleared these works away, to Pinkus's great indignation. Clegg & Samuda claimed to be the rightful patentees, but Pinkus resisted this, though Clegg had in fact improved the original system. Eventually the West London directors agreed to allow Clegg & Samuda to carry out trials, and these used a single line, from three chains south of the Great Western main line to the Uxbridge Road, commencing on June 11 1840. Although attended by members of parliament, engineers such as Brunel, Prince Albert and "a fair proportion of the fair sex", the trials were inconclusive, and the West London directors showed no interest in purchasing the equipment, which was eventually removed in 1843.

In March 1845, the little company gave up its attempt to operate the West London line, and it was leased to the LNWR and the Great Western for 999 years. The latter company made little use of it, as there was no running junction with their main line, but the London & Birmingham which was absorbed by the London & North Western Railway in 1846, did send some freight trains, mainly of coal, to Kensington. But entrepreneurial imagination foresaw that if extended, the West London could become the nucleus of a useful cross-Thames route to the railways of South London. In 1859 the LNWR and the Great Western, together with the London & South Western and the London, Brighton & South Coast, promoted the West London Extension Railway, the LNWR and the GWR contributing £100,000 each, and the LSWR and the LBSCR £50,000 each towards the £300,000 share capital. The WLER took over the Kensington Canal which had been purchased by the BBTJR in 1839 and turned most of it into a railway which extended the WLR through West Brompton and Chelsea. Continuing across the river it connected at Clapham Junction with the LSWR and the West End of London & Crystal Palace Railway, by which the LBSCR gained access to their new terminus at Victoria. The extension was opened at the beginning of March 1863 as a mixed gauge line; the GWR beginning to run broad gauge trains into Victoria from April 1.

There were also connections with the London Chatham & Dover Railway at Longhedge Junction, and later with the District Railway via Earls Court Junction, just south of Addison Road, and East Kensington Junction west of Earls Court.

The West London Extension Railway climbed by an incline to gain height for its bridge over the river, making a level junction with the LSWR. Its connections with the LBSCR and the LCDR took the form of branches which passed under the LSWR. Stations were opened at Chelsea & Fulham and at Battersea; West Brompton being added in 1866. Thus the little West London was transformed into a valuable link between the main line railways north and south of the Thames; not only did local services using this route multiply, but later long distance expresses such as the "Sunny South Special" also used it.

When the Hammersmith & City Joint Railway from Paddington to Hammersmith was opened on June 13 1864, a short spur was included from Latimer Road to the West London Railway at Addison Road, and this gave the GWR access to the WLR and via the West London Extension line into Victoria, where the LCDR and the Great Western leased part of the premises, two tracks being laid with mixed gauge rails. From 1 April 1863, the GWR operated a broad gauge service from Southall via Acton, North Pole Junction and Battersea (WLER) to Victoria; this continued until March 22 1915, when, like many cross-London services, it fell victim to wartime stringency. In 1869 the LNWR began a service from Broad Street and Willesden to Victoria (LBSCR) which also used the West London line; this survived until 1917.

There was also a short-lived attempt to use the Paddington–Victoria via West London link for long distance express trains; during the summer of 1906 a Paddington–Brighton service was introduced, using LBSCR engines and stock, but this failed to attract custom. A sort of reciprocal arrangement came when a service from Birmingham (Snow Hill), GWR, via the West London into Victoria, with one train each way daily, commenced on October 1 1910, but this, too, succumbed due to lack of demand and was withdrawn in 1911.

On February 1 1872, the LNWR began to operate a service known as the "Outer Circle". This ran from Broad Street over the North London Railway to Camden Town, the Hampstead Junction Railway to Willesden Junction and thence via the West London and West London Extension Railways to the District Railway via a connection at Kensington East Junction, terminating at Mansion House.

On August 1 1872, the Great Western started a half-hourly service called the "Middle Circle", of trains from Moorgate initially (but from Bishopsgate from July 12 1875 and from Aldgate from December 4 1876) to Mansion House, via the Hammersmith & City Railway, the Latimer Road curve, the West London, the WLER and the District. Like the Outer Circle, this was not a true circle; leaving a gap between the Mansion House and Aldgate. The Outer Circle was particularly circuitous, though it may have had some use for passengers from the north western suburbs travelling to the City, prior to 1880 when the Metropolitan opened to Willesden offering a swift alternative.

Congestion on the District Railway caused the Middle Circle service to be cut back to Earls Court on July 1 1900, and on 1 January 1905 it was further truncated to terminate at Addison Road, becoming the responsibility of the Metropolitan Railway. The Addison Road spur was electrified on 1 January 1907, enabling the service to be electrically worked by a 3-car train of H & CR stock. Later, when paths east of Baker Street were required for Extension Line trains, the Addison Road service became a shuttle from Edgware Road, or sometimes only from Ladbroke Grove, with one of the two single, self-contained compartment motor coaches, Metropolitan Nos 46 and 69, sharing the work with H & CR stock. After the latter was withdrawn during 1936 this duty was taken over by ex- District Railway "C" Class stock, built in 1911. On October 19 1940, however, the spur from Latimer Road to the West London line was seriously damaged in an

BUSY DAY – ADDISON ROAD ON 26 AUGUST 1933

Mixed goods rumbles through southwards behind LMS '7'F 0-6-0 9507.

Edgware Road bound Hammersmith and City line train.

Ramsgate portion of the 'Sunny South Express' heads south behind 'D1' 1743.

Photos: H. C. Casserley

air-raid, together with Uxbridge Road station, and the shuttle service was withdrawn, never to reopen.

LNWR steam trains on the Outer Circle service continued working through to Mansion House; from December 6 1905 steam traction gave way to District Railway electric locomotives at Earls Court, but from January 1 1909 the service terminated at the latter station, probably because of congestion on the District tracks eastwards. The West London and the WLER had been electrified; the LNWR tracks from Kensal Green Sidings to Uxbridge Road Junction were converted in 1913/14 as part of the North Western's wider London electrification scheme, and from May 1 1914 a daily service of electric trains between Willesden High Level and Earls Court began, initially using trains hired from the District Railway.

The LSWR's new Kensington and Richmond Railway line from the WLR from just north of Addison Road to Hammersmith (Grove Road) opened on 1 January 1869 and is described in our EAST TO WEST THROUGH HAMMERSMITH section.

A scheme known as the Metropolitan & South Western Junction Railway was proposed and received its Act in 1872; this was intended to carry the District from West Brompton across the Thames to Barnes and a joint station with the LSWR. But the District's finances were insufficient to push this scheme through. However, they did succeed in extending their line for one mile from West Kensington Junction to Hammersmith Broadway.

This was opened on September 9 1874, and it only needed a further 39 chains of new railway to take the District up to a junction at Studland Road with the LSWR's new line from Addison Road to Richmond. A bargain was struck with the Midland Railway, who promised in 1876 to pay 4% on the £350,000 needed for this short connection; in exchange the Midland were offered coal yards at High Street and West Kensington on the District, together with the use of Earls Court as a terminus for a St Pancras service. This never materialised, but the MR did get a goods and coal depot, reached by a 40-chain branch from West Kensington.

So the District Railway at last reached Richmond, which seems to have been a veritable Mecca for Victorian railway promoters, and they started a service to that station on June 1 1877; it soon attracted large numbers of passengers and has continued to do so.

Not so happy is the story of the LSWR line from Addison Road to Hammersmith Grove Road. Using the spur at Grove Road, the Metropolitan began running a service from Aldgate to Richmond on October 1 1877; the GWR had already commenced running in 1870 between Bishops Road and Richmond; this was resumed in 1894, and henceforth trains of both these companies could be seen at that town. When the Hammersmith & City Railway was electrified in 1906 the Grove Road spur was excluded from the programme. After this only Great Western trains ran through to Richmond over the Kensington and Richmond metals; a GWR steam rail-motor service continued until 1910. Wartime conditions exacerbating competition from the Central London with its station at Shepherds Bush, and by District electric trains to Richmond, rendered the KR redundant and it was closed on May 5 1916.

The station at Shepherds Bush, opened in 1874, was still standing in forlorn abandonment in a patch of waste ground eighty years later, but the surviving canopies and platforms have now vanished under a block of high-rise flats.

In the late 19th century family holidays became very popular, and resorts in the south of England were very much favoured by people in the Midlands and the North. But for a whole family with its vast amount of luggage to change trains and cross London by cab meant much strain and inconvenience. The West London and West London

Extension provided a very good way to obviate this, and the London & North Western and the London Brighton & South Coast companies introduced through carriages between Liverpool and South Coast resorts, which travelled via Willesden Junction, where an LBSCR locomotive took over and worked the coaches forward to Addison Road and on to Brighton or Eastbourne via Clapham Junction.

Some services from the LNWR to the LBSCR at East Croydon had been running as early as 1863, and a Kensington to Brighton summer service was operating from 1863 to 1874 and from 1882 to 1904. The famous "Sunny South Special" was first introduced in July 1904 with through carriages from Liverpool, Manchester and Birmingham to Brighton and Eastbourne, running as a separate train on the LNWR from 1 March 1905, with additional carriages to serve Deal, Folkestone and Dover added from July of that year. It was formed of LNWR coaches, as at that time the LBSCR did not possess any vestibule carriages. There were several variations in the stations served by the "Special"; for the northbound working a stop at Rugby was included, where the Birmingham carriages were detached, and the remaining through coaches were attached to the Liverpool and Manchester portions respectively of the 14.40 express from Euston.

Another through north to south service via the WLR and WLER was that of a through SE & CR coach from Deal to Liverpool introduced in July 1905; this was altered to run to and from Manchester in July 1908. Wainwright designed some very handsome tri-composite coaches for this service which were vestibuled. I shall not attempt to describe fully the complex and varied through north-to-south workings via the West London and WLER, but they were reinstated after the Great War, a conflict which had imposed great strains on the WLR and WLER route. During mobilisation of the British Expeditionary Force in August 1914 servicemen were collected from railway stations all over Britain, and by the end of the month 670 troop trains arrived at Southampton, bringing over 118,000 soldiers for embarkation for overseas, not to mention 22,000 horses, 2,400 guns and quantities of stores. A large proportion of the vast military traffic which came from the Midlands and north of England and continued throughout the War passed over the vital Addison Road link.

These troop trains from the north passing through Addison Road seem to have bred a sense of mystery, and there were rumours of a Russian army, "with snow on their boots", passing through England. Hamilton Ellis suggests that this may have come about when a troop train from Scotland halted at Addison Road and a porter, hearing a conversation in Gaelic, and in a supposedly foreign language, asked "Ere, where d'you come from?" "Ross-shire" replied a weary voice inside the carriage. "Blimey, Bill" said the porter to a colleague, "Rooshans!" Writing in the "Railway Magazine" in July 1939 Ellis mentioned that at that time the rebuilding of Addison Road station was expected. Sitting in the big refreshment room on the east side, he said, with its huge Victorian fireplace, black cat, purplish rugs and friendly, musical barmaid, you could easily imagine yourself fifty years back in the past.

However, in September 1939 war once more cast its shadow over the West London and the WLER, and long cavalcades of carriages filled with servicemen passed through Addison Road, freight trains too. The station's long platforms and easy access made it especially suitable for movement of large numbers of passengers; it was used for the evacuation of schoolchildren, and it was made railhead for 18 London hospitals in evacuating patients. Special troop trains were run from September 9 to October 5 1939, to move the first contingents of the British Expeditionary Force to their ports of

Casualty – the remains of Uxbridge Road station (closed in 1940) looking north west.

Kensington Olympia 1988 once again a great vantage point for a variety of trains. The banner erected by North London Railways during its brief existence could benefit from laundering . . .

. . . the station is dominated by the great roof of Olympia which could well be the canopy of a railway terminus itself.

?H.C. Casserley

*Former LBCR 'D1' 0-4-2T No B 629 leaving the West London
Extension railway at West Brompton with a train for Clapham Junction.*

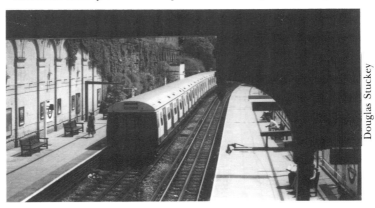

Douglas Stuckey

*Seen from under the canopy of the Underground station a District
train for Wimbledon departs on a sunny afternoon in 1999.*

Douglas Stuckey

*Phoenix rising! A Silverlink 315 set departs for Willesden Junction
from the reconstructed WLER station soon after reopening in 1999.*

embarkment, many via the West London line, but, though the long distance holiday trains were withdrawn, normal local passenger services were maintained at first. But in May 1940 the retreat from Dunkirk began, and from May 27 until June 4 all normal services were cancelled, to make way for many troop trains carrying soldiers from the Channel ports full of weary soldiers evacuated from France. On May 31 and June 1 this traffic reached its peak, with 107 and 110 special trains respectively, nearly half of which were worked north via the West London line. By the end of the operation 319,056 troops had been evacuated, British and French.

The blitzkreig brought its victims too; Addison Road was hit several times, and the connection from Latimer Road on the Hammersmith & City line to Addison Road was closed after bomb damage on October 19 1940; Uxbridge Road station was also badly damaged. The "Sunny South Special" luxury trains disappeared, their paths needed for urgent traffic. Among much additional military material handled by the West London line was mail for the Canadian forces, which had previously been handled at Manchester Mayfield Road.

Bombs fell on several West London and WLER stations; on West Brompton station on the night of October 9/10; this failed to explode but stopped traffic until it could be disarmed. By the end of that month St Quintin Park station had been destroyed, Addison Road was hit four times, and Battersea station was burned out.

At the end of 1941 it was decided, in fear of invasion, to clear from a southern coastal belt some 30 miles deep every kind of material and stores which the enemy might use, and once again this burden fell on the West London and WLER. In 1944 preparations for the D-Day invasion began, and here once more the West London line played a prominent part. In the first phase 24,459 special trains were needed to move stores and troops; on May 10 the second phase involving the transport of 7,000 tanks on 800 special trains, and finally, three weeks before D-Day, 9.679 trains were run to carry the mass of the troops. A large proportion of these southbound special trains were routed via the West London line. Traffic continued to be very heavy after the invasion; for instance, soldiers' mail demanded three long trains a day from Nottingham via Addison Road to Dover, a figure which grew to 16 as Christmas drew near. From June 1944 a new menace appeared with flying bombs, and a few months later a more refined missile, the V2 rocket, added to the danger.

So at the end of the war the West London and West London Extension Railways were in no state to restore passenger services, with Addison Road battered and roofless, and other stations in various states of decay or bomb damage. It was not until 1949 that it was possible to route north-to-south long distance services via the WLR and WLER, and these were almost entirely Saturday only services. The luxurious trains of pre-war, with their ex-LNWR restaurant cars and multi-directional destination boards were things of the past; in these austerity post-war days many of the southbound runs were made at night, with the same set of coaches returning north later that same day. There was an interesting revival in May 1979, when a twice-daily service was introduced between Manchester and Brighton, via Birmingham, Reading, Old Oak Common and the West London line. These trains were initially non-stop from Reading to East Croydon, though a brief stop was made at Kensington to change trains crews and this later became an advertised stop. A service had continued to run between Clapham Junction and Addison Road for the benefit of Post Office Savings Bank employees who worked at Blythe Road, Kensington. For many years it did not appear in the public time-tables as its operation varied to suit the requirements of the Savings Bank and it had the distinction of being the last surving steam operated local service in the London area. It was finally dieselised in 1967.

There were several goods depots on the West London Extension Railway. The LNWR and the GWR both had depots reached by short branches running northwards on the east side of the line from near West Brompton, the GWR facility being known as Warwick Road Depot. The North Western's Brompton & Fulham Depot was situated about a mile further south on the opposite side of the railway. Also reached via the WLER was another Great Western goods depot at South Lambeth on the SECR at Battersea and the LNWR at Clapham Junction had a goods depot. Coal from the north of England was a staple element of freight traffic to all these depots, as was milk; Addison Road was an important staging point for the marshalling of loaded and empty milk tanks to a variety of depots in the London area. But sadly this revenue was gradually lost to British Railways after the five-week long ASLEF train drivers' strike in 1955; this forced the dairies to use road haulage instead, and so although some milk traffic returned, it was gradually lost to rail, and within twenty years had disappeared completely. There was also a significant traffic of Lyons' cakes from their factory at nearby Cadby Hall. The GWR, and later Western Region, also carried meat containers from the GWR depot at Smithfield Market to South Lambeth and other GWR depots reached via the West London and WLER.

Of the intermediate stations on the West London Extension Railway, Battersea and Chelsea & Fulham opened in 1863, and West Brompton opened three years later, all succumbed to falling traffic and wartime stringency, closing in October 1940. St Quintin Park & Wormwood Scrubs on the West London rather fell between two stools, not being really convenient for either of the districts claimed by its title. It was set on fire by an incendiary bomb and burned down on October 3 1940, never being reopened.

The end of World War II found Addison Road station in a sad state as a result of bombing and arrears of maintenance. London Transport introduced a service of shuttle trains from Earls Court, on December 19 1946, in connection with Bertram Mills Circus at Olympia, and these ran for other important exhibitions, using the sound end of the down platforms as their terminus, but this meant twice crossing the down main line, so in November 1947 a platform face to the disused Southwest bay line was built. Later, in 1958, an independent single line was built through the spare arch of Addison Bridge; this gave direct access to the London Transport lines.

More radical rebuilding was very necessary, however, and the station buildings on both sides were dismantled, the west side being first dealt with beginning on June 12 1958. The Northwest bay was completely rebuilt, with its two lines increased to four, to prepare for its new role as a Motorail terminal, with the area enclosed by a large shed. A small new concrete station building was erected on the site of the old down side building, and was opened on May 24 1966. Alterations to give an independent route for District trains to Earls Court have been mentioned; these entailed many alterations to track layout, which were carried out in February and March 1958; the former down main line now became a siding, with the former up main line reserved for down working; a former siding to the east of it now became the up main line.

The Motorail terminal had four platforms and, under its new name, Kensington Olympia became the central point for all British Railways' car-carrying services to and from London, all bookings being dealt with there, including those for the Eastern Region Caledonian Road to Perth service. Other Motorail services included Kensington to St Austell, Dover to Newton-le-Willows, Newhaven to Stirling, and Stirling to Dover, which was described by the BBC as the longest Motorail service in the British Isles. But after the 1982 summer season the terminal was closed and the services were diverted. This may have been because it was at one time intended to redevelop the station, as the London terminal for Channel Tunnel services; but it was not to be, and Waterloo was chosen instead.

On May 12 1986, the Inter-City Sector increased the through north and south service to six southbound and seven northbound. Northern terminals included Manchester, Liverpool and Birmingham, and the southern ones were Dover, Brighton and Newhaven; all these trains called at Kensington. At the same period the West London and WLER remained a very important route for freight trains, some twenty-eight daily workings being booked to pass through Kensington, with even more running on certain days.

Royal trains have used the West London and West London Extension Railways on several occasions. The first was on December 10 1870, when Queen Victoria travelled from Windsor to Watford, the Royal train reversing at Kensington, where the LNWR pilot and train engines took over. On November 23 1875 the Royal train, travelling from Ballater to Windsor, had to be diverted from its scheduled route because of floods, and was switched to the West London for reversal, this time at Shepherds Bush, where two GWR engines took the train on to North Pole Junction. On May 25 1898, the body of W. E. Gladstone was brought from Hawarden Castle, his home in Flintshire where he had died, to Westminster via Earls Court Junction, and carried from the District Railway platform to Westminster Hall where he lay in state. The private subway built by the District for the Houses of Parliament was used for access. Another occasion when a celebrity's remains were conveyed over the West London route was on January 30 1928, when Earl Haig's funeral train, consisting of two carriages and a van hauled by ex-LSWR "M7" 0-4-4 tank engine E106, was worked from Waterloo to Willesden. The Field Marshal was buried in Dryburgh Abbey, near Melrose, so the train was presumably handed over to an LMS engine at Willesden Junction and taken forward via the West Coast Route, Carlisle and the Waverley Route to Melrose station.

A great variety of locomotive types have worked over the West London/WLER route over the years, from the LMS and its constituent companies, the Great Western, constituents of the Southern Railway, and even a Glasgow & South Western engine and Hull & Barnsley 0-6-0s on loan to the SE & CR during the Great War. LNER locomotives were rarer visitors because that company had no direct connection with the West London route, but they were not unknown especially from the Great Central line. Electric multiple-units have included LNWR Siemens and Oerlikon saloon trains, Metropolitan and Hammersmith & City saloon stock of 1905/6, and District trains of various vintages on the Earls Court–Olympia service. In 1936 a Great Western diesel parcels railcar used to collect cakes and confectionery at Addison Road station from J. Lyons & Co at Cadby Hall, for distribution to Lyons depots at Reading and Oxford.

Electric traction returned to the British Railways tracks on the West London line with the construction of a depot at North Pole to serve the Channel Tunnel Eurostar services, which also saw the reinstatement of the chord from Latchmere Junction to West London Junction on the LSWR main line. The lines from Clapham Junction (Western) and (Central), Longhedge and West London Junction were electrified at 750v dc Third Rail as far as Mitre Bridge Junction linking with the 25kv ac overhead electrification of the West Coast main line. North Pole Eurostar depot was also electrified at 25kv.

This lead to the Clapham Junction to Kensington peak hour service being electrically operated from July 1993. However, from 29 May 1994, after years of pressure from local politicians, an all day service was introduced between Willesden Junction (High Level) and Clapham Junction and until the short section from Mitre Bridge Junction to Willesden Junction was electrified in 1996 this was operated by diesel multiple units. From 1 June 1997 a further new service was introduced from Gatwick Airport to Rugby by Connex South Central, using dual voltage Class 319 electrics: this was one of the first initiatives by the newly privatised railway companies. These services have been so successful that West Brompton station was rebuilt and opened in May 1999, and there are plans for a new station at White City to form part of a vast regenerative plan for a shopping/leisure/transport complex in the area.

District R38 stock on an Exhibition train arrives at Kensington Olympia March 24 1976.

Buses

Hammersmith, both as a fast burgeoning community and as a crossroads from all directions, was chosen as the terminus of many early bus services.

As early as 1707 a daily coach from the Bell Inn in the Strand to Hammersmith was advertised, but travel by road was generally more expensive and less comfortable than a boat on the River. In 1830 within a year of the historic London debut of the omnibus introduced by George Shillibeer, a Mr George Cloud was offering a Hammersmith–City bus service via Shepherds Bush, his vehicles brightly painted in red with knifeboard seats.

In 1839 horse-buses were licensed to ply from Hammersmith to broadly "near city" destinations – Leadenhall Street, Mile End Gate, Bank and Whitechapel Church, and many others passed through Hammersmith from Kew Bridge and other termini. From 1853 omnibus proprietors began to see (and feel!) that unfettered competition – "a free choice between several rotten oranges" – spelt economic disaster, and learning from the French experience with a controlled monopoly of omnibus services in Paris, and with French leadership, many eventually acquiesced in the formation of, and sold out to the *Compagnie Générale des Omnibus de Londres* – the London General Omnibus Company, which had no monopoly but became over the years at least *primus inter pares* and the leader in the Capital's bus world. 22 Hammersmith-based buses were purchased by the LGOC in 1856.

Soon after this acquisition an R. F. Miller of Hammersmith, (probably a carriage-maker working in King Street), won an LGOC prize for an improved design of omnibus – his innovations provided better ventilation and access to the upper deck by steps with handholds rather than the daunting ladder rungs which until then had faced the "outside" passenger.

Among the various horse bus services of an early date were two railway-operated by the Great Western and Metropolitan Railways as feeders to their Hammersmith and City line. In 1875 a service was commenced from Shepherds Bush station to Turnham Green, it was diverted to run from Hammersmith in June 1876, but withdrawn from 18 February 1878, after the District and Met trains had started to run to Turnham Green over the LSWR in 1877. Two days after the closure of the Turnham Green service on February 18 1878 a new route from Hammersmith to Barnes was introduced with three one-horse buses. Two-horse buses were the order from 2 April 1888, and they ran until these feeder services finished on 30 April 1899. Some penny fares were available undercutting LGOC buses which had a fairly expensive minimum two penny fare.

The first service of the new London Road Car company formed in 1889 was from Hammersmith to Victoria; its buses had "garden" seats facing forward as opposed to the knifeboard upper deck then usual on its competitors vehicles, and they flaunted a Union Jack which emphasised their patriotism against the "Frenchy" origins of the LGOC.

The internal combustion engine did not immediately become the successor to the horse-bus. Electric, petrol-electric and steam power were tried on some considerable scale. A strange looking Thorneycroft steam bus with an alarming coal or coke-fired

LGOC Horse Bus waiting to start the long trot to Liverpool Street from Turnham Green.

Hounslow Cultural and Community Services: Local Studies Collection Chiswick Library

A converted Horse Bus body was used to build this Thornycroft Steam Bus used by the London Road Car Co Ltd for a short period from March 17 1902.

A much more elegant and modern-looking Steam Bus, a Clarkson double-decker which commenced service on September 5 1905.

boiler and tall chimney was let loose on a Hammersmith–Shepherds Bush–Oxford Circus route in 1902, but within two months it had out-stayed its welcome.

In March 1904 the LGOC put a Clarkson steam bus on to a Piccadilly–Hammersmith service but this lasted only for a loss-making fifteen months; likewise the Road Car Co's two similar steam buses put again on a Hammersmith–Shepherds Bush route at the same time were equally unsuccessful. A 26 seater electric bus of the London Electric Omnibus Co., in March 1898 had made a return journey from Trafalgar Square to Hammersmith in an hour and three quarters including a stop-over of 17 minutes. But the short time for which an electric vehicle could operate without recharging or servicing meant that for economical sustained public transport it was impractical (and so, unfortunately, it largely remains today). Eventually the petrol engine proved far and away the most efficient and reliable of the new mechanical modes of traction, and the development of motor bus services accelerated. The competition between tram, train and bus became fierce and often to no-one's lasting benefit, and, in due course, the LGOC, the Underground Group and LUT trams were united, (the LGOC with the Underground Electric Co., in 1912) and one aim of the union was to 'reduce the omnibus competition in areas where competition . . . is most rife, and to employ omnibuses taken off such routes for opening up new districts where the omnibus can fulfil what the railway interests describe as its most important function, that of feeder to fast electrically-operated suburban train services.' Inter-ticketing arrangements were to be encouraged. (An illustration of the massive effects of competition between modes is that when LUT trams reached Hounslow, the LSWR lost 64% of its receipts at that station, despite fighting the newcomer by the provision of more steam trains). The unification and co-ordination of London's passenger transport took long years of controversy and complex negotiations, through the London Traffic Act of 1924 to the formation of the London Passenger Transport Board. In the early 1920's independent bus proprietors launched what were popularly always known as "pirate" bus services – the first of this generation of "pirates" was introduced by A. G. Partridge on 5 August 1922, on perhaps London's best-known route – No 11 – from Shepherds Bush to Liverpool Street. Under the jolly name of "Chocolate Express" (never more than six vehicles) they operated successfully until 1934, when they were absorbed into the LPTB. A. G. Partridge was a respected transport man who became Chairman of the Independents' Association and their capable spokesman.

Over the years close to two dozen different premises in Hammersmith were used as bus or tram depots. A host of independent operators tried their luck in the area at various dates – the "Omega", "Universal", "Monarch", "Eclipse", "Gleaner" and many more challenged the big boys, often on the major routes such as Numbers 9 and 11.

The area of Hammersmith and West London had been a hub of bus activity since buses first appeared on the streets, and the LGOC underlined its importance in the bus world when in 1922 it opened the famous Chiswick Works to "centralise the overhaul of buses and the overhaul and conditioning of bus parts and units." To quote further from London Transport's Golden Jubilee Guide of 1983 – "By the 1950's with the gradual increase in the size of the bus fleet as they steadily replaced the trams which were overhauled separately at a works at Charlton, there was a need to expand the bus overhaul facilities. Thus in 1956, a large new factory was opened at Aldenham for the overhaul of bus bodies and chassis, releasing more space at Chiswick for the increasing demand for reconditioned and overhauled mechanical and electrical units – the engines, gear boxes, starter motors and so on." Chiswick was the bus training centre with its spectacular skid-pans, home of the Research Laboratory, the Supplies Centre including uniforms for the whole of the LT train and bus operation. During an Open Day of the 1983 celebrations there were "opportunities to ride on the skid bus during certain of its demonstrations." One wonders if the Health and Safety Executive would sanction such rides today! In 1979 LT employed 2680 at Chiswick but in 1988 the Works closed and discussions about the permanent future of the large site still continue. The nearby bus garage at Turnham Green, which originated as an LGOC horse bus garage in 1899, closed in 1980 and the vehicles and staff transferred to the elegant former works and HQ of London United Tramways at Stamford Brook, now the depot of London United buses which have a large share of the bus provision in the Hammersmith area. Other operators at the time of writing are – Armchair, Ealing Buses, Limebourne, London Country, London General, MTL London, Thorpe's and Westlink.

The LGOC also had garages at Wells Road, Shepherds Bush (now a second London United Garage) by Goldhawk Road station, and Hammersmith (Riverside) at Hammersmith Broadway. Riverside Garage was built in 1913 and incorporated in its Queen Street (Queen Caroline Street) frontage the "fine garden facade" of 18th Century Bradmore House, gaining the garage one of the few honourable Hammersmith mentions in a Royal Commission of Ancient Monuments in 1925!

Riverside garage closed in 1983, and its operations moved to Shepherds Bush and Stamford Brook in preparation for the major redevelopment of the whole area and the construction of the new bus station, opened in October 1994, on an island site above the new District and Piccadilly Underground station described elsewhere, with access from the station and adjoining shopping mall by escalators. The oval bus station building cannot be entered by foot on the level, only by bus or up the escalators. There is an enquiry kiosk and cafeteria; sloping roadways controlled by traffic lights allow vehicle entry or exit from and to Hammersmith Road and Talgarth Road.

The opening of a very large bird and wildlife sanctuary, The Wetland Centre of Barnes, on the south bank of the River, coming into being partly through the negotiations some years back of the late Sir Peter Scott, is intended to be served by a substantially subsidised (£600,000) bus service linking it with Hammersmith and Barnes stations. Inevitably the Press has already christened this the "Duck Bus".

'B' type with No. 11 destination board at London Transport Museum

A British Airways Routemaster, one of 65 used on a Heathrow service from 1966 to 1979, shown here stabled at the former LUT tram depot.

London United Bus Garage, Goldhawk Road, Shepherds Bush, 1999.

Douglas Stuckey

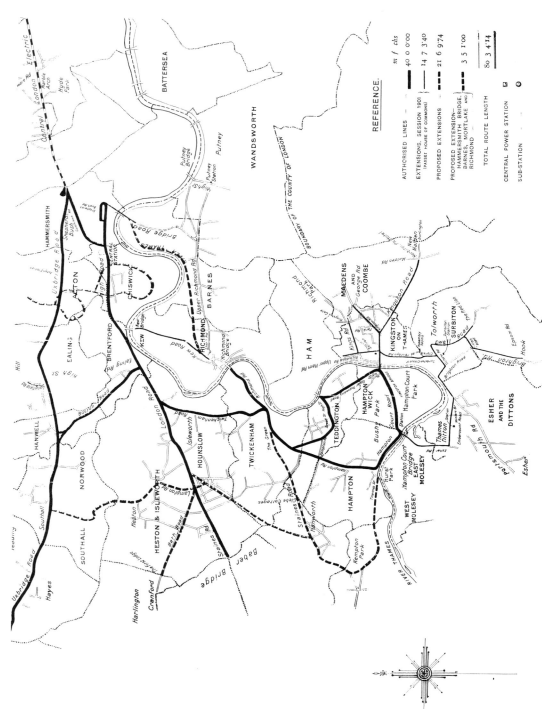

London United Tramways map 1901 at the height of its power and ambitions.

Trams and Trolley Buses

As we have said, the first omnibuses were neither very cheap nor very comfortable; the first tramcars (horse drawn) came on to the streets of London in the 1860's, and trams proved to be longer-lasting, more capacious and less costly in operation. Hammersmith's first acquaintance with tramways occurred in 1870 with the formation of the Southall, Ealing and Shepherds Bush Tram Railway Co. Ltd, but this company, bedevilled by the restrictions of official red tape and lack of cash soon ran into trouble and initially managed to build only one mile of line from Uxbridge Road station to the Princess Victoria, Askew Crescent. A lessee, C. C. Cramp took over the business and in September 1875 resumed running as far as Askew Crescent. The firm of Reid Bros. in 1878 purchased the original line and had secured authority earlier by the Shepherd's Bush and Priory Road, Acton Tramway Order of 24 July 1876, to continue the SESB line from Askew Crescent to Acton Lane. On 14 November 1878 was registered the more substantial, innovative but still sorely under-financed West Metropolitan Tramways Ltd which in its turn acquired both the SESB and SBPRA.

An Act of Parliament of 10 August 1882 authorised WMT routes from Hammersmith Broadway to Kew Bridge, from Shepherds Bush down the Goldhawk Road to Young's Corner, and a separate service from the south end of Kew Bridge to Richmond. The then Kew Bridge was considered too steep and narrow for safety. By 1898 the WMT, in its turn, was facing financial nemesis and attempts to secure support were not helped by reports such as that in the September 1894 "Railway World"; "The local authorities have maintained . . . that when their officials have returned from an early morning stroll, laden with debris of the permanent way in the shape of pieces of rail 3 or 4 feet long, they were justified in holding that the tramways in their streets were unquestionably a nuisance and, as such, should be removed".

George White, Chairman of Bristol Tramways, was appointed receiver and he supervised the WMT's absorption into his own Imperial Tramways Group. On 19 July 1894 a new company, London United Tramways Ltd was registered to take over all the WMT routes, depots at Chiswick, Richmond and Shepherds Bush, 49 trams and hundreds of horses. The depots were described as: "Chiswick . . . (just off Chiswick High Road, between the present Merton and Ennismore Avenues), with stabling for 140–170 horse, a 3-storey granary, fodder stores sheds for 20 cars, seven cottages . . . a yard and an exercise ground. Shepherds Bush Depot (between Shepherds Bush Road and Wells Road) with stabling for seven pair-horse cars".

The LUT was unable to develop tramways to the east, towards the heart of London, as it was blocked by the decision in Kensington, by the newly-formed borough and previously by its predecessor the Vestry, to prohibit tramways within its borders. Eventually this encouraged the energetic LUT to become involved in schemes for tube railways, and so into the Underground Group, driven by the ruthless American, Charles Tyson Yerkes.

The LUT operated the first electric tramcars in London, and they were handsome and comfortable enough for Clifton Robinson, the charismatic managing director of LUT who ran his company with some style and panache, to state to a Royal Commission on London Traffic: "I have no sympathy for the archaic bus – it is an anachronism and is looked upon more-or-less as a fit object for a museum not for public transport." This was true enough when comparing electric or even capacious horse-trams with horse buses, but this was in 1905 and the first motor-buses were coming onto the streets in large and competitive numbers. The limitations of horse-power were early evident to tramway proprietors and WMT experimented with a battery-powered converted horse car, but it seems that promises that the batteries would sustain operation for seven hours with a load of 46 passengers were more than optimistic! It is said to have run for one day only – March 10, 1883. In 1888–90 WMT gave trial to another form of mechanical traction, the Litoff closed-conduit system, on a stretch of track at their Chiswick depot but this proved too complex and vulnerable. The LUT eventually decided to electrify all their routes using overhead wire conductors, but the newly-formed London County Council forbade this in their constituent borough of Hammersmith as elsewhere. So horse trams had to continue until 4 April 1901, when permission had at last been granted for all services, except Kew Bridge to Richmond which remained horse-drawn until its demise a decade later.

Following the formation of the LCC in 1888 the new Council almost immediately moved into the field of tramway operation, using its powers to purchase and develop London's systems. An LCC depot was established at Hammersmith to the east of the Met. District station and separated from it by the tiny dwellings of Hanover Cottages. The LCC double track swept across the Broadway from Brook Green in the north, and down Fulham Palace Road, whilst the LUT's separate single terminal loop ran round the triangle formed by Beadon Road, King Street and the Grove. By 1908 LCC cars were running south east to Putney Bridge, and north to Willesden and Wembley. The LUT and LCC tracks at Hammersmith were not physically united until 1922, when the LCC bought all the LUT tracks within Hammersmith borough boundaries, although LUT cars continued to work through to their Hammersmith and Shepherds Bush termini. LUT had spread its tentacles widely westward, using at times the legal provisions for light railways which prevented a great deal of the possible opposition from local authorities, and the LUT's development is summarised in Barker and Robbins' "History of London Transport"—

> "Clifton Robinson's patient negotiations with the local authorities eventually secured the powers he needed along the route of the two existing horse routes to Acton and Kew Bridge, and also, pressing further west, along the Uxbridge Road from Acton to Southall and beyond Kew Bridge to Hounslow, agreement on the Hounslow route being reached in February 1898 and on the Southall route three months later. He also secured powers to Uxbridge under the Light Railways Act. He then went on to secure further concessions beyond these limits down to Twickenham, Kingston, Hampton Court and the Dittons, and round to the Maldens, Wimbledon, South Wimbledon, and Tooting, though these sections of the network were to be opened in later stages, between 1902 and 1907".

THE LONDON UNITED TRAMWAYS.

MR. BALFOUR ON RAPID TRANSIT.

There were many places in which Londoners yesterday sought to evade the smiting rays of the July sun, but none in which the attempt was more successful than upon the electric tram-cars which signalised the opening by the London United Tramways Company of the first completed section of the system of electric tramways. The long line of tramcars—as imposing as a Lord Mayor's procession—was drawn up in a shining array by the Shepherd's Bush terminus, and one by one these saloons of velvet and twinkling brass slipped away with a hiss of triumph over rails which stretched away seven miles to Acton, Ealing, and Southall. Hundreds of people watched the triumphal procession go by; there were arches to welcome the visitors at Uxbridge Road, and at Ealing, where the new departure coincided with the incorporation of Ealing as a Chartered borough, there were speeches and celebrations to signalise the double event. The tram-cars sped—at a rate and with a smoothness to which most tram-cars are strangers—through leafy lanes and the last remnants of what remains to Middlesex of her rural scenery, and then turned to come back by other lanes and shaded ways until Hammersmith was reached. Here in the electric power station, where festoons of roses hung in charming but incongruous contrast with the mighty machines and sleepless dynamos, a lunch was given, at which the chairman of the company (Mr. White) presided over an assemblage of several hundred visitors.

On the chairman's right was Mr. A. J. Balfour, on his left Lord Revelstoke and Earl Grey; and others who were present included Lord Rothschild, Lord Herries, Sir Edward Reed, Sir William Preece, Sir Benjamin Baker, Sir John Kennaway, Mr. P. J. Watson, Dr. Silvanus Thompson, Dr. Fleming, and Mr. Yerkes. The toast of "Success to the Company" was proposed by Mr. A. J. Balfour.

Mr. Balfour remarked that the questions of crowded cities and of the congestion of districts could always be stated in terms of power and cost. If it were possible to move from the outermost suburbs of a great city to its interior, at no cost,

and at a speed which made the distance negligible, there would be no question of congestion; and hence the future of the great question of overcrowding must be solved in its largest details by companies such as these which grappled with the questions of swift and cheap locomotion. Questions of compensation for disturbance and re-housing and the like did not touch the heart of the problem; the real problem was the best means of establishing communication between the inside and outside area of London. He stopped for a moment to point out that every means of better locomotion thus established by tramways put a greater strain on the means of connection—the streets and their traffic—

in inner London, and pointed out that this was a question which the future would not be able to shirk. But meanwhile he would draw attention to the fact that the number of passengers which it was estimated that the completed tramways would carry was at least 150,000,000 in the year, and he would point to that, not merely as a matter of local or commercial, but of national interest, as a matter affecting enormously the comfort, happiness, and civilisation of the community.

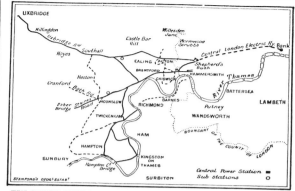

WEST LONDON'S ELECTRIC TRAMWAYS: MAP SHOWING THE EXTENT OF THE PROPOSED TRAMWAYS.

WEST LONDON'S ELECTRIC TRAMWAYS: THE OPENING OF THE FIRST COMPLETED SECTION.

From the Daily Graphic *July 11 1901.*

Hounslow Cultural and Community Services – Local Studies Collection
Chiswick Library

INAUGURAL PROCESSION, CARS PREPARING TO START

Inaugural procession cars preparing to leave Shepherds Bush at the opening of London United Tramways electric services.

Courtesy Frank Goudie

LUT eight-wheeled double-deck cars type 'U2'.

Left: *Car 267 on route 89 to Acton outside Hammersmith (H & C) station.*
Right: *Car 286 on route 57 to Hounslow outside Shepherds Bush (CLR) station with entrance arch to White City on right.*

The LCC cars running north from the Broadway carried destination boards reading somewhat curiously "near Willesden Junction". This was because Willesden Junction station was almost entirely in Hammersmith, and thus within the county of London, but the section of Harrow Road leading to it from Scrubs Lane was in Willesden and, therefore, outside the LCC perimeter.

Tramways had for long more rigorous regulations than buses – fixed stopping places, no standing passengers and so forth, and local councils had demanded and secured for themselves expensive road-widening and bridgework before assenting to new routes. LUT always had to endure a litany of complaints about noise, (the grinding of wheels at corners, the clanging of bells), unpunctuality and the fall in property values!

Proposals by the Central London Railway to turn itself into another "circle line" and to penetrate LUT territory had led Clifton Robinson to say "We shall have to go in for tubes ourselves". "What do we know about tubes?" asked George White. "What we don't know we can learn", replied Robinson.

In co-operation with the formidable and ruthless American financier, Pierpoint Morgan, who was scheming for tube railways in north and central London, the LUT deposited a Bill in November 1901 to incorporate a London United Electric Railways Company whose projected tube lines were: Barnes to Charing Cross via Hammersmith, Kensington, Hyde Park Corner and the Mall; a loop from this line at Hammersmith to Brook Green Road, Shepherds Bush, Holland Park and rejoining at Kensington, and Marble Arch to Clapham Junction. But Robinson fell out with Morgan, and smoothly facilitated the passage of LUT to the Underground Group of which the afore-mentioned Yerkes, another American not over-dainty in any aspect of his life, was the driving force.

As early as 1911 Chiswick council applied successfully for powers to build a "railless traction" route in a loop from the High Road along Chiswick Lane, Burlington Avenue . . . and back to the High Road, but the powers were never exercised. By the late 1920's the disadvantages of the traditional tramcar with its fixed middle-of-the-road (or otherwise obstructively placed) rails in the increasingly crowded and chaotic London streets became intolerable. LUT began experimenting with trolleybuses in Wimbledon, and the subsequent success of LUT's conversion from tram to trolleybus of its Kingston area routes in May 1931 convinced the newly-born London Transport in 1933 to decide on a programme for the complete replacement of the tramway system which it had inherited.

Trolleybuses took over on most of the Hammersmith/Shepherds Bush tram routes in 1935/7 – Shepherds Bush to Hounslow, and Hammersmith to Hampton Court on 27 October 1935, Shepherds Bush to Uxbridge on 13 December 1936; Craven Park to Clapham Junction, and Harlesden to West Croydon, both via Hammersmith, on 12 September 1937.

The era of the trolleybus was brief. The LUT had put into service 60 six-wheel vehicles of rather angular appearance, known affectionately (and otherwise) as the "Diddlers"; in 1936 LT introduced a much smoother-looking and very comfortable bus with 74 seats and much larger than the contemporary motor bus. Although the LT trolleys all had a recognisable outline with over 1700 vehicles in the fleet, LT did not standardise and there was a number of different styles and makes, each having its own classification.

Although the trolleybus was popular for its quiet and comfortable ride, the 1939–1945 war emphasised the advantage of the bus's flexibility over the trolley, forever shackled to its overhead wires. On 15 November 1946 LT announced that diesel buses 'being eminently suitable and much cheaper' would take place of the 800 trams still in service.

March 1959 saw the beginning of the end for the trolleybus. In July 1960 the change came to Hammersmith with the cessation of trolley operation out of Hammersmith depot, and the introduction of buses on four routes. It had been intended to retain the Hammersmith routes until later, but the construction of the Hammersmith flyover which would have involved rewiring expense, and the wish of British European Airways to have the depot as a base for their LT operated Heathrow Airport buses hastened the process. In November 1960 went the long route from Shepherds Bush to Uxbridge, and Hanwell to Clapham Junction, and in January 1962 the routes north to Edgware and Finchley. A final farewell to the trolleybuses took place on 8 May 1962 when the last routes from Hammersmith to Hampton Court, and Shepherds Bush to Isleworth gave place to the ubiquitous omnibus.

A handsome reminder of tramway days is what was LUT's dept and power station at Stamford Brook, tucked away just off the High Road. This is now the head office of London United buses, and the buildings seem not only in remarkably good shape after nearly a hundred years, but the design of the sheds themselves would be dated by a uniformed observer as certainly no earlier than the nineteen thirties. Part of the power station is now converted into flats and much of the elegant interior appointments and ironworks have been preserved.

LONDON UNITED TRAMWAYS LIMITED.

INTERIOR VIEW OF CAR.

Special Saloon Car

To Seat 20.

s. d.

Rate.—7/6 Return for each 1d. of the Ordinary Fare.

Example :
TWICKENHAM TO HAMMERSMITH.
Single Fare by Tram   -   -   -   4d.
Return Fare for the complete party by
Special Car   -   £1 10 0

This Car can be engaged by parties visiting theatres, concerts, balls and other —— social festivities. ——

Shepherds Bush tram terminus and "Twopenny Tube" station. It is not clear what event produced the unusually large congregation.

A "Diddler" – one of the fleet introduced by LUT and the first trolley buses in London.

Hammersmith Bridge with former central pier.

LCC Penny Steamer "Earl Godwin" 1907.

P. Drake-Brookshaw's poster for the 1937 Boat Race.

London Transport Museum

76

Boats – But Not in Winter

London and its authorities, perforce or chance, have always used the Thames – a largely God-provided free highway – for the transport of people and goods. As early as 1817 (some sources aver 1813) steam in the shape of the "Richmond" and "London" "yachts" began plying between Blackfriars and Richmond.

"In its fifteenth year the Hammersmith Bridge company conceived a pier of its own to augment the tolls. Paddle steamers were calling at Barnes Pier, a short wooden jetty at the White Hart, in 1840, and plying as far as Margate. Tierney Clark and the secretary found the barge *Sukey* suitable for conversion at Blackfriars in February 1843 when Mr A. Adams brought it up river to Hammersmith for 3s. It was moored off shore parallel with the Barnes bank, attached to the masonry pier of the bridge at one end and to a piled dolphin at the other, with stairs down to it from the downstream footway. Passengers objected to a double toll, a penny on the pier and a halfpenny on the bridge, so that in September 1843 a notice was posted:

> The Hammersmith Bridge Committee have ordered that all persons crossing the Bridge to or from the Company's Pier shall pass TOLL FREE."*

The building of Bazalgette's new bridge in the 1880's deprived Hammersmith of its pier for a period and following a 'memorial' representing the wishes of "a population of 105,900" and asking for their steamboats back, a new pier was built closer to the Barnes bank in 1894.

However, "the Thames rarely provides the shortest distance between important points; and the rise and fall of the tides is substantial, which creates considerable berthing and scheduling problems. Moreover, in London weather, travel by river (given a choice) is a highly seasonal affair," so by the 1880's railway development on land had caused a serious decline in waterborne passenger transport. Despite this the idea of a viable river passenger service did not die, (and has not done up to today) and perhaps the most ambitious project came in 1905, with the inauguration of a London County Council municipal fleet of purpose-built craft; the Act of Parliament authorising the new service provided for passenger and parcel traffic between Hammersmith and Plumstead with fares at a penny a mile, and a new pier built at Hammersmith to accommodate the LCC steamers, and named Hammersmith Town Pier to distinguish it from the bridge pier. The bridge pier itself lasted until 1921 when it was demolished.

The first workman's boat from Hammersmith left at 5.00 am and from 7.00 am there was a fifteen minute interval service; at certain times "express boats" left for London

---

*from "Hammersmith Bridge" by Charles Hailstone, (Fulham and Hammersmith Historical Society, 1987).

Bridge, calling at Putney, Battersea, Nine Elms and Westminster. Through fares with the LCC tramways were also available . . . but all in vain . . . by 1908 the loss-making steamboats ceased operation, after a change of party in power at County Hall.

Nothing daunted by earlier lack of success, proponents of "river buses" were extremely active in the 1930's led by that indefatigable Thames man, Sir Alan Herbert. In 1933 he published "No Boats on the River" and in pursuance of his campaign invited in 1938 the Speaker of the House of Commons to visit him by water at Hammersmith. "The Times" related that it being half-tide he had to be decanted into a dinghy and marched through the mud.

'APH' as Sir Alan was affectionately known, lived at Hammersmith Terrace, where a plaque records his residence. After the Hitler War in which this man of many (including naval) parts signed up as a petty officer in the river patrols protecting the Thames, he returned to the advocacy of passenger transport on the River. After an adverse London Transport report in 1946, casting doubt on its feasibility, he joined forces with R. G. Odell who took possession of a boat-building yard at Walton on Thames and built a number of stylish boats, capable of carrying 150 passengers each. A water bus service from Kew downstream was opened with a colourful ceremony on 7 July 1948 but Hammersmith was omitted from the stopping places.

After some rather unco-operative argie-bargie between the various river interests but a degree of profitability for the water buses, in 1951 the Thames Passenger Boat Operators Association marshalled the available river fleet to provide intensive services for the Festival of Britain.

These consisted of:

1) A pier to pier service of water buses between Hammersmith and Greenwich.
2) Express services as needed between the Festival Piers on South Bank, Battersea Park and other places.
3) A shuttle service between the South Bank Exhibition and Battersea Pleasure Gardens.

Through a number of changes of route and policy the water bus service came to an end in 1962.

The current Hammersmith Bridge has been shut twice for longish periods for all but public transport, owing to doubts about its structural strength. Soon after its most recent reopening it was for the second time, in May 2000, a target for bombers, presumed to be dissident Irish republicans.

The White City

The White City was a brainchild of Imre Kiralfy and his brother Hungarian impresarios, who had already made their mark substantially in the world of entertainment with nearby Olympia and Earls Court. The project was a massive gamble when in 1908 140 acres were laid out at Wood Lane for a Franco-British exhibition, the largest exhibition held in Britain up to that time. The land had been leased from the Ecclesiastical Commissioners, and in addition to the exhibition halls and gardens the White City sports stadium was erected as a home for the 4th Olympic Games, also held in 1908. There were 40 acres of white stucco-coated buildings and half a mile of waterways.

A principal and popular feature was the Canadian or Mountain Scenic Railway: "A trip on the railway was equivalent to a visit to Canada or the United States, and the visitor could enjoy a wonderful journey . . . One mile of track was built and the distance was crammed with every style of scenery that could be met in any part of the world . . . mountains and valleys, lakes and rivers, caves and grotesque waterfalls . . . The journey was on one of the comfortable electric trains powered by the generators in the machinery hall, and while travelling it would reach a speed of 50 mph, and through an elaborate system of signals preventing any possibility of a collision or accident . . . When the Exhibition closed over 2,800,000 passengers had been carried with receipts of £70,000."

"Rides" were a great and popular feature of the Exhibition . . . in addition to the Scenic Railway there was "the Canadian Toboggan", a cross between switchback and toboggan giving an exhilarating trip from a high platform over an undulating track and finishing with a steep last incline; there was "the Spiral" where in "comfortable cars" one made an helical journey to a high altitude and a similar descent; and there was too "the Mountain Slide" a sensational development of the "Helter Skelter" which gave "the pleasurable sensations of the mountaineer's glissade." At first visitors were carried around the grounds in "trains" of three carriages pulled by petrol-engined trucks, but in 1912 their place was taken by an electric tramway running close to the perimeter but whose layout appears to have been modified over the years.

The White City was opened on May 14 1908 by the Prince and Princess of Wales (soon to be George V and Queen Mary), shortly afterwards King Edward VII escorted the French President on a visit, and on August 21 the young princes, Albert and Edward, turned up with their tutor and had four rides on the scenic railway and, as is rather curiously emphasised, purchased Maynards toffee . . . which must have been gratifying for Maynards.

An adult day ticket for the Exhibition was 1/- with an additional charge of 6d on the amusements. Writers have expressed different opinions as to whether this price was cheap enough to encourage the working classes or whether the White City remained a largely middle class-dominated resort. In October, newspapers and the South Eastern and Chatham Railway sponsored cheap travel for people from Kent to visit the White City; a typical cost was 4/- rail fare from Canterbury and a reduced price entry ticket at 8d.

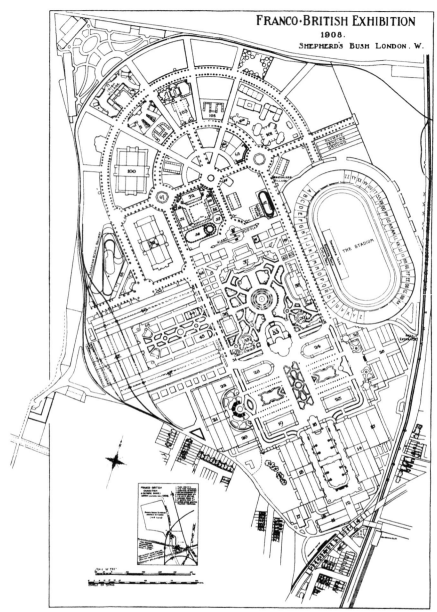

FRANCO·BRITISH EXHIBITION
1908.
SHEPHERD'S BUSH LONDON. W.

Halls 1 to 9, on the east side of Wood Lane, adjoining Shepherd's Bush Station.

10. Entrance from Wood Lane (new stations on Central London and Hammersmith and City Railways adjoin).
11. Instruments of Pure Science.
12. Musical Instruments — Fancy Articles.
13. Palace of Industry (British).
14. Palace of Industry (French).
15. Education (British).
16. Congress Hall.
17. Administrative Building.
18. Custom House.

19. Applied Art (French).
20. Popular Café.
21. Palace of Decorative Art.
22. French Restaurant.
23. Applied Art (British).
24. Palace of Women's Work.
25. Sports Club.
26. Fine Art Palace.
27. Lagoon Restaurant.
28. Palace of Music.
33. Imperial Pavilion.
35. Pavillon Louis XV.
36. Franco-British Pavilion.
37. Grand Restaurant.
38. Garden Club.
39. Royal Pavilion.

44. French Artisans' Pavilion.
45. Paris Municipal Pavilion.
47, 48, 49. Machinery Halls.
50. Canadian Palace.
51. New Zealand Pavilion.
52. Crown Colonies Pavilion.
54. Spiral Slide.
55. The Spider's Web.
57. Toboggan.
86. Old London.
100. Australian Palace.
101, 104. French Colonies.
102. Ceylon Tea House.
103. India.
105. Indian Tea House.

Following the closure of the Franco-British exhibition, for several years the White City reopened each summer with a different theme. During the Great War the White City area was mostly taken over by government, and the buildings used for the production of war materials, and by the time that peace came many halls were derelict. Post-War saw no great revival of the White City's fortunes and on Tuesday 7 November 1922 the White City was put up for auction whilst the lease still had 82 years to run.

A revival came at the stadium in 1927 with the introduction of greyhound racing, and for a spell (1931–33) the stadium acted as home ground to Queen's Park Rangers FC. Because of cash shortage in the past, QPR have "changed ground on no fewer than 16 occasions, far more than any other club in the Football League." In 1917 they took over the ground of disbanded Shepherds Bush amateur club at Loftus Road, and there apart from 1931–3 they have remained. By 1978 five exhibition halls were still standing which were used for a variety of purposes, from insurance offices to tennis and racquets courts; the landlord by then was British Rail. BR had hopes and aspirations for the site and when the proposal for a Channel Tunnel first showed renewed signs of life, suggested that the ground be used as a goods terminal which could be linked efficiently with the Kent coast.

As early as 1949 the BBC, with foresight, acquired 13 acres of the former White City. Here rose the Television Centre from which the first programmes were broadcast on June 29 1960. The TV centre was finally completed in 1996.

Many an entrepreneur has looked at Wood Lane and hoped to start a phoenix from the ashes of dereliction lying there. In 1990 Balfour Beatty secured local planning consent to build one of the largest shopping centres in London there, rebuilding Wood Lane Central depot at basement level and restoring the ornate arch close to Shepherds Bush Central Line station. Unfortunately, this phoenix did not fly but, as we write, a plan for a new White City is being submitted by Chelsfield's which again entails a substantial part of the inital expenditure being devoted to reconstructing Wood Lane depot under cover and a little to the west of the existing layout. £150,000,000 would be allocated to major work on the Central Line and other infrastructure needs, and the whole scheme for "enormous range of beautifully designed spaces, filled with exciting shops, restaurants, cinemas, galleries, libraries and gardens" is intended to be served by new bus and tube facilities, (and possibly a station on a rejuvenated WLR), eliminating the need for large-scale private car access.

The Author and Publishers are substantially indebted to Donald R. Knight and his booklet "The Exhibitions – The White City" for much of the information in this section. Any readers with a particular interest in the subject can forward any comments or questions for Mr Knight c/o the Publishers.

The stadium in 1908.

Douglas Stuckey

The White City Main Entrance.
Left: *Glory days 1908.*   Right: *The glory has departed 1998.*

The Television Centre in Wood Lane opened in 1960. The BBC bought the 13 acre site (which was part of the home of the 1908 Franco-British Exhibition) in 1949.

BBC

A typical early spectacular at Olympia.

A
WORLD OF
ENTERTAINMENT

The 'Palais' – once a Mecca for servicemen on leave – has had many 'lives'.

Loftus Road – home of Queens Park Rangers FC and the Wasps Rugby Club.

Douglas Stuckey

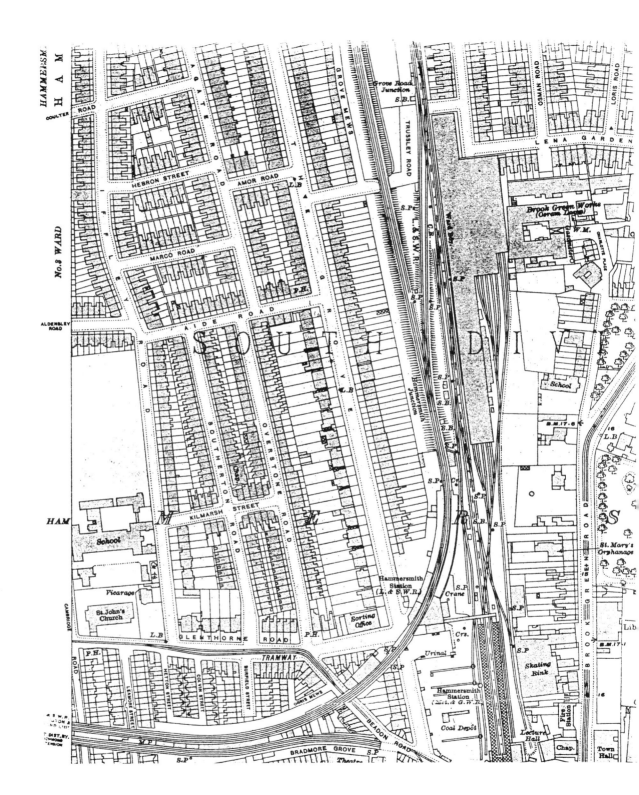

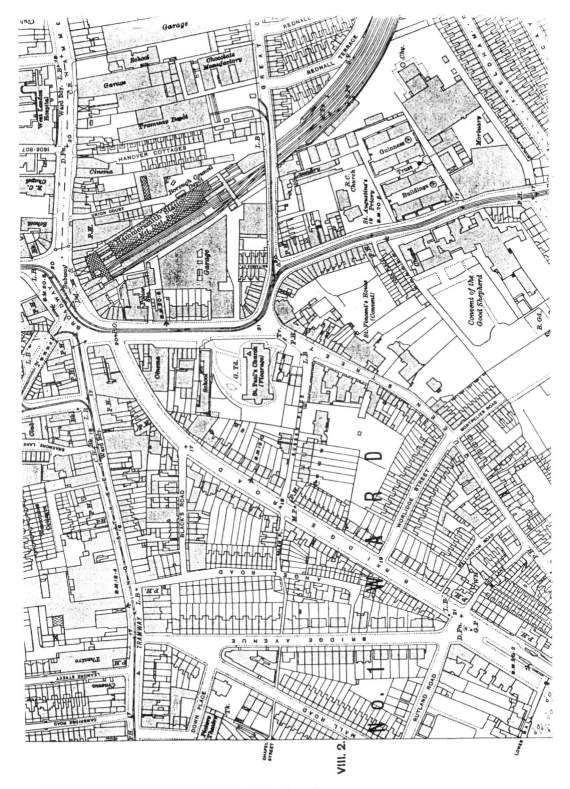

HAMMERSMITH AT THE TIME OF THE 1914–18 WAR.

Opposite: Above the Broadway.
This page: The Broadway and below.

85

Taken from the Ordnance Survey
by kind permission.

A Selection of Tickets

HAMMERSMITH AND CITY

LONDON & SOUTH WESTERN – SOUTHERN RAILWAY–BRITISH RAILWAYS

CENTRAL LONDON – EALING & SHEPHERDS BUSH

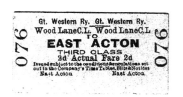  

PICCADILLY

DISTRICT

LONDON PASSENGER TRANSPORT BOARD

LONDON TRANSPORT EXECUTIVE – LONDON TRANSPORT BOARD – LONDON UNDERGROUND

Acknowledgements

The Author and Publishers wish to thank sincerely the people and organisations who have helped us with this book.

Unfortunately it is impossible to name them all individually but they include: The Libraries and Librarians of Hammersmith, Chiswick and Kensington, the Greater London Record Office, Mr John Shelbourn and the Transport Ticket Society, Mr David Clift and the Fulham and Hammersmith Historical Society, Mr Nicholas Moss and the BBC, the London Transport Museum, Mr Peter Harding and Mr Brian Morrison.

Some sources of information

Chiswick Past, Gillian Clegg, Historical Publications, 1995.

The Exhibitions – Great White City, Donald R. Knight, 1978.

Farewell to London's Trolleybuses, Michael H. C. Baker, Ian Allan, 1994.

Great Western London Suburban Services, Thomas B. Peacock, Oakwood Press, 1970.

Hammersmith and City Railway Board Minutes.

Hammersmith and Fulham Through 1500 Years, Leslie Harker, Fulham and Hammersmith Historical Society, 1992.

A History of Hammersmith, Hammersmith Local History Group, 1965.

A History of London Transport, (Vols 1 & 2), T. C. Barker and Michael Robbins, George Allen and Unwin, 1974.

The London & South Western Railway, (Vol 2), R. A. Williams, David & Charles, 1973.

The London & South Western Railway in the Twentieth Century, J. N. Faulkner & R. A. Williams, David & Charles, 1988.

London's Local Railways, Alan A. Jackson, David & Charles, 1978.

London's Lost Railways, Charles Klapper, Routledge & Kegan Paul, 1976.

London's Tramways, John Reed, Capital Transport, 1997.

Metropolitan District Railway Board Minutes.

Metropolitan Railway Board Minutes.

Metropolitan Railway General Manager's Papers.

The North London Railway, Michael Robbins, The Oakwood Press, 1974.

A Royal River Highway, Frank L. Dix, David & Charles, 1985.

Seventy Years of the Central London, London Transport, 1970.

Underground Railways of the World, O. S. Nock, A. & C. Black, 1973.

West London Joint Railways, J. B. Atkinson, Ian Allan, 1984.